THE
LITTLE GIANT® BOOK
OF
Whodunits

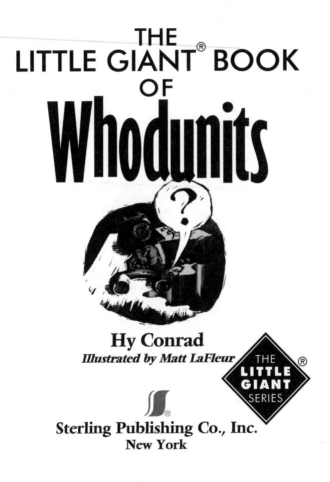

Hy Conrad
Illustrated by Matt LaFleur

Sterling Publishing Co., Inc.
New York

Edited by Jeanette Green

Library of Congress Cataloging-in-Publication Data

Conrad, Hy.
    The little giant book of whodunits / Hy Conrad ;
illustrated by Matt LaFleur.
      p.   cm. — (The little giant series)
    Includes index.
    ISBN 0-9069-0473-9
    1. Puzzles. 2. Detective and mystery stories.
3. Literary recreations. I. Title. II. Series.
GV1507.D4C6673   1998
793.73—dc21   98–6165
                                       CIP

5   7   9   10   8   6   4

Published by Sterling Publishing Company, Inc.
387 Park Avenue South, New York, N.Y. 10016
© 1998 by Hy Conrad
Distributed in Canada by Sterling Publishing
c/o Canadian Manda Group, One Atlantic Avenue, Suite 105
Toronto, Ontario, Canada M6K 3E7
Distributed in Australia by Capricorn Link (Australia) Pty Ltd.
P.O. Box 704, Windsor, NSW 2756 Australia

Manufactured in Canada

Sterling ISBN 0-8069-0473-9

CONTENTS

Who Killed Santa Claus? 7

Agent Brown's Shining Moment 10

Super Bowl Madness 14

The Vanishing Love Token 18

Friends at the Office 22

Death of a Deceiver 26

The Party's Over 30

The Smuggler and the Clever Wife 33

The Suicidal House Guest 37

Looking for a Lookout 41

High-Rise Homicide 44

The Coach's Last Play 48

Long-Distance Murder 52

The Queen Glendora Photos 55

The Dirty Cop 59

The Stolen Cleopatra 63

Archie's Christmas Surprise 67

Postgraduate Murder 71

The Last Poker Hand 74

The Pretenders' Ball 77
Good-Neighbor Policy 81
Killer Camp Food 85
Eye Spy 89
The Piney Bluffers 92
The Vandalizing Visitor 95
An Attack of Gas 99
An Inside Job 102
The Convent Mystery 106
Death by Chocolate 110
A Quali-Tee Theft 114
The Three Stoogles 118
The Shortcut Robbery 122
The Locked Room 125
A Timely Alibi 129
A Chinese Lie Detector 133
The Brothers Ilirium 136
The Pre-Valentine's Day Murder 139
A Real False Alarm 143
Airport Insecurity 146
The Pretenders' Ball, II 149

A Winter's Tale 152
Strangulation Station 156
The Suicidal Schemer 160
A Theatrical Threat 163
A Hard Day's Night 167
Myra's Three Sons 170
A Nun Too Pretty Murder 173
Three Weak Alibis 177
Bye-Bye, Bully 181
Maria's Last Clue 185
The Telltale Prints 188
The Kidnapping Killer 192
The Gypsy Thief 196
Chili con Carnage 200
The Playboy's Empty Vase 203
The Emery Emerald 207
The Bad Samaritan 211
Tornado Allie 214
A Housewarming Theft 217
Which Dewdit Did It? 220
The Pretenders' Ball, III 224

The Nutty Strangler 228

Hand in the Cookie Jar 231

Around-the-Clock Murder 235

The Pretenders' Ball, IV 239

Driven to Suicide 242

Even Hypochondriacs Die 246

The Penguin House Murder 250

The Flat Motorist 254

The Clumsy Thief 258

Welcome Back, Cutter 262

The Videotaped Suspect 266

A Maid-Made Discovery 270

Fooling the Foolproof Alarm 274

Death in the Woods 278

Murder Works Overtime 282

Two Places at Once 286

Dead-End Stoolie 290

A Lapse in Security 294

Alibi at Sea 298

Whodunit Solutions 301

Index 350

Who Killed Santa Claus?

It was midnight on Christmas Eve when the maintenance staff of Kimble's came to work in the deserted department store. When they arrived at the North Pole display, they discovered every child's worst nightmare, the lifeless body of Santa Claus. He was in a storage room, his head bashed in by the butt end of a .44 revolver.

Santa's off-duty name was Rudolph Pringle. "That's Rudolph's revolver," the manager informed the police. "He started carrying it after a six-year-old pulled a knife on him."

"Do you know anyone who would want to see Rudolph dead—besides the six-year-old?"

The manager cleared his throat. "Santa's been having a lot of fights with his elves. I know three elves who'd threatened to kill him."

The detective had the murder weapon bagged. Then he placed it on the center of the interview table, right where the suspects would be forced to

6½

6

5½

5

look at it. "Rudolph Pringle has been murdered," he informed each elf. "What do you know about it?"

Joe Winters shivered and couldn't stop staring at the gun. "I know nothing. Some of the guys had trouble with Rudolph. But he was always nice to me. I left the store at nine, right when it closed. I was too tired to change, so I wore my costume home. No one said a word on the subway."

"Rudolph was a pig," snarled Sam Petrie, the second elf. "If he pushed me too far, I wouldn't smash his head in. I'd sue. What's the use of a dead Santa when a live one can be made to pay?"

Robert Goldstein was the smallest elf. On hearing the news, he burst into tears. "Last week, Rudolph started a fight. He said I was too slow bringing in the kids. He slapped me on the head and called me all sorts of names. But I didn't kill him."

The detective called in his assistant. "Well, we have our killer," he said with a smile. "All I had to do was use a little psychology."

Whodunit?

Solution on page 348

Agent Brown's Shining Moment

A black Cadillac tore around the busy street corner, barely slowing as it approached the steps of the courthouse. The tinted, passenger-side window rolled down and a semi-automatic handgun poked its barrel out.

Pauly Gillespie, mob informant and federally protected witness, stood frozen in his tracks, his worst fears looking like a definite possibility. Pauly's FBI bodyguards threw themselves on top of him, but not before two shots erupted and Pauly had taken a bullet in the shoulder.

The Cadillac screeched across two lanes of traffic. But it made the mistake of turning left down an alley and getting stuck behind a double-parked delivery van. The two hit men scrambled out and raced away—right into the arms of four off-duty officers. Having heard the shots and the sirens, the

officers grabbed the running men and held on until the FBI caught up.

Special Agent Brown was new to this unit and was always given the boring, inconsequential jobs. In this case, he was told to clear the Cadillac out of the alley so that normal traffic could resume. Brown adjusted the rearview mirror, backed the car out, and drove it around to where his colleagues were Mirandizing their suspects.

Brown stood and watched. One of the handcuffed men was tall, lean, and sullen. The other was a good five inches shorter, Agent Brown's height. Large but short. He spoke animatedly, gesturing freely with his hands.

Agent Fordney, director of the unit, seemed exasperated. "They ditched the gun back in the alley," Fordney growled. "They ditched their gloves back there, too. All right, boys, I'm going to ask you again. Which one of you was the shooter?"

"Not me," said the large, short man.

"Not me," said the lean, sullen one.

Agent Brown smiled. Here was his chance to

impress his boss. "I know who the shooter was," he said softly.

Who was the shooter and how did Agent Brown know?

Solution on page 301

Super Bowl Madness

Vince McCormick was a big, angry slug of a man just a month shy of retirement. On Super Bowl Sunday, his two sons, Vince Junior and Sonny, came over as usual to watch the game.

As kick-off time approached, the boys were in the kitchen, helping their mother prepare the snacks. Junior heated up nachos in the microwave while Sonny poured the bags of potato chips and pretzels into bowls. Marie McCormick was mixing the ice and ginger ale and rye together in tall glasses.

"Make sure mine is strong enough," came her husband's growl from the living room.

Junior saw the bruise on his mother's arm. "Did he do that to you?" he asked. Marie didn't answer.

"What'll you do when he retires and hangs around all day?" Sonny asked. "It'll only get worse."

"No one in our family gets divorced," Marie said firmly. "Oh, dear. I forgot which is your father's. Taste the highballs, Sonny."

Sonny tasted the drinks, nearly choking on the third one. "It's about twice as strong as the others."

"Give it to me." Vince was suddenly standing right behind them, grabbing for his drink. "Making me come in here," he muttered dangerously. Sonny carried in the snack bowls while Junior took in the nachos, just in time for the kick-off. Marie followed with the other drinks.

All four sat around the T.V., munching on the snacks and sipping their drinks. It was near the end of the first quarter when Vince Senior held up his empty glass. "Get me another," he bellowed.

Marie was in the kitchen working on the refill when she heard a gasp, then a moan. She returned to find her husband crumpled in his easy chair, dying.

"A strong, fast-acting poison," the homicide detective said. "Two to five minutes. And yet they all claimed to be eating the same things. They're obviously lying, covering up for each other."

"Not necessarily," a sergeant ventured. "It

could've happened just the way they said."

How could Vince have been poisoned? And who could have done it?

Solution on page 340

The Vanishing Love Token

The Valentine's Day party was a tradition. Each year Henry and Bitsy Vandercleef invited their friends into their Park Avenue home. After a sumptuous dinner, the couples retired to the drawing room. The men drank port, the women drank champagne, and each couple exchanged love tokens.

This year George Epson outdid himself, presenting his wife with a ruby necklace. The women sighed enviously while the men mentally added up the cost and wondered how their wives would react to their own less extravagant gifts.

When Henry's turn came, he told Bitsy to close her eyes and led her over to the windows. When Bitsy opened her eyes, she saw the billboard and gasped. "To Bitsy, the most beautiful woman in my world. Love, Henry."

"You don't know how much trouble it was getting a billboard put up on Park Avenue," Henry

said. The women sighed again while the men mentally added and wondered.

George Epson was the first to notice the missing necklace. "Stolen," he gasped, holding up the empty jewel box. "Nobody leave the room."

Everyone assured everyone else that there couldn't possibly be a thief among them. Not them. The necklace must have fallen out or been mislaid.

Systematically, they searched the room. There was nothing in the empty champagne bottle. Nothing on the thick Persian carpet. The crystal decanter set was in place and all the containers filled to the top with whiskey, port, and bourbon. The glasses were examined, as were the folds of the red tied-back curtains flanking the locked windows. They even inspected the red crystal chandelier.

"What about the dog and cat?" Henry asked. The butler quickly rounded up both pets, stuck his fingers down their throats and then checked out their favorite hiding places.

In desperation, all the guests permitted themselves to be searched. Still nothing.

Police Inspector Clyde, the poorest member of the gathering, finally spoke. "It does look like robbery," he said reluctantly. "And while I don't know who took the ruby necklace, I can tell you where it is now."

Where is the necklace? And how did Inspector Clyde know?

Solution on page 346

Friends at the Office

Homicide Detective Gilson was visiting his accountant in a small, seedy office building when he heard noises coming from above. First there were angry voices. Then came a scream, followed by a heavy thud.

Gilson excused himself and raced up the stairs. On the next floor, he found an open door. Wiley Kline, a low-rent lawyer, lay on the floor of his office, a switchblade knife sticking out of his chest. Gilson called in the murder and immediately found himself assigned to the case.

When his partner arrived, the detectives examined the office. Not far from the victim's hand was a half-smoked cigarette. On the floor beside it were a turned-over wastebasket, a cheap lighter, and a blank notepad. On the desk they noticed a telephone, a pen, a shot glass smelling of bourbon, and an ashtray filled with cigarette butts and burned matches.

"It's funny how none of his neighbors poked their heads out," Gilson observed. "Let's go talk to them."

The floor contained three other offices. The first door they knocked on produced Helen Hurly, a massage therapist. She told them she was relaxing between appointments. "I didn't hear a thing," she claimed, pointing to the stereo headphones she'd just removed. "You say Wiley was murdered? I'm not surprised. He must have cheated everyone he'd ever met."

The second office belonged to Jackson Cod, an artist. In one hand he held a paintbrush, in the other an unlit cigar. "Sure I heard the scream. But I was right in a moment of inspiration. Besides, you hear all sorts of things in this building." Jackson held out his cigar. "Either of you fellows got a light?"

Behind door number three was Lionel Wafer, a chiropractor, also between appointments. "I heard a scream. What happened?" Gilson told him; then he asked Lionel why he was holding an ice pick. "Oh. I'm defrosting," Lionel said and returned to the old, ice-ladened refrigerator in the corner.

"You want a drink or a cigarette? We should cele-brate. Kline deserved what he got."

Later, the detectives compared notes. "Well, we definitely have a suspect," Gilson said.

Whom did Gilson suspect and why?

Solution on page 316

Death of a Deceiver

Mona Fisher turned and gazed at Jerry, sleeping next to her on the plane. Her eyes wandered down to his wedding band. She still couldn't believe she was married to such a catch.

Their flight from Acapulco landed late that night. The next morning, February 10, Jerry Fisher shoveled the snow from the driveway, kissed Mona good-bye, and headed off to work.

At seven that evening, a cleaning woman entered the law offices of Fisher & Dyce and discovered the body of Jerry Fisher. He had been stabbed to death, a sharp letter opener still sticking out of his chest.

Lieutenant Miller's first unpleasant duty was to interview the young lawyer's widow. Mona was distraught. "We were only married four months. I never met a man more romantic and honest. Why would anyone want to kill him?"

Jerry's law partner, Kyle Dyce, echoed her senti-

ments. "Jerry was a man I trusted completely, and a darn good lawyer. He was still working when I left. About 6 P.M. I walked across to the health club. I didn't work out, just used the tanning bed. I suppose I was jealous of Jerry's great Mexico tan."

The lieutenant spent the next hour going through Jerry's papers and discovered that the trusted Jerry Fisher had been skimming money from the law partnership. He also found the phone number of a woman—Gail Lowenski.

They located Ms. Lowenski just leaving the art gallery she managed. The attractive redhead was devastated by Jerry's death and even more devastated to hear that he'd been married. "We were together just this afternoon, at my apartment. The louse told me he was single. For two months he was stringing me on. I was so sure he was going to propose."

Lieutenant Miller and his partner showed up to witness Jerry Fisher's autopsy. "All three of them had motives," the partner whispered as they stared down at the cold, naked body. "The only trouble is, they didn't know they had motives."

"One of them knew," Miller said. "And I know which one."

Whom did the lieutenant suspect and why?

Solution on page 311

The Party's Over

Tony had promised to help clean up after the party and Tony was a man of his word. Still nursing a hangover, Tony dragged himself over to Fernando's house. The two men had coffee, then walked into the fenced-in yard, scene of last night's birthday revels.

The lawn was strewn with blown-up balloons and bottles and streamers, but after an hour of work, they managed to get it cleaned up.

"Darn," Fernando said, pointing up to a tree by the edge of the eight-foot-high wooden fence. A balloon was stuck in a top branch. "I'd wait for a breeze to blow it off, but there hasn't been a breeze in days."

Fernando climbed the tree. He was just a few inches from knocking free the balloon when he glanced into a window of Gil Dover's house next door. "Looks like a robbery," he yelled down. "Broken window. A big mess. Tony, my phone's not working. Go to the corner and call 911. I'll meet you by Gil's rear gate."

When the police arrived, Tony and Fernando were waiting outside the splintered gate to Gil Dover's backyard. "That's how we found it," Fernando explained. "We didn't go in." Upon entering, the police found what Fernando had said: a broken window, a big mess in the den—plus ten missing rare coins worth $100,000.

Gil Dover wasn't too disturbed. "The coins were insured," he reported. "My uncle left me the collection, and frankly I'd rather have the money. I usually put the alarm on. But today's cleaning day. I don't put it on when the house cleaner comes."

But the cleaner had never come. Al, of Al's Domestic Service, was at his own house across town. He said he got a message from his answering service asking him to skip this week.

A sergeant checked his notes. "Dover says he left home at his usual time, 11 A.M. Fernando looked over the fence at 11:30. Anyone could have broken in during that half-hour period."

"Maybe," his captain replied. "But I have a good idea who's responsible."

Whodunit and how?

Solution on page 329

The Smuggler and the Clever Wife

A Mexican border guard was talking to his wife over his cellular phone when he accidentally pulled in a fragment of a static-filled conversation between a man and a woman. "I'll be waiting in Tecate at noon for your regular Monday shipment," said the man. "You don't think the border guards are getting wise?"

"No," the woman laughed. "We can keep this operation going forever." And then, just as suddenly as they'd come, the voices disappeared.

For a full month, customs officials kept track of the traffic at the relatively quiet border crossing. Only three women made a regular habit of crossing into Mexico each Monday morning.

The first woman, impeccably dressed, drove a black Mercedes. The second, a girl barely out of her teens, always crossed on an old red bicycle.

The third drove a small van. "MexiCoast Spa" was on the side in fancy letters. Of the three, she was the only one declaring merchandise, a weekly supply of U.S.-made health foods and vitamins on which she paid a hefty tariff.

On the fifth Monday, they detained all three women. Methodically they searched, tearing every panel from the dark blue Mercedes, even checking inside the tire tubes. They did the same with the bicycle. Searching the van took the most time. Luckily, this week's shipment of health food was smaller than usual. The officers took samples from every box and bottle.

After finally allowing the women into Mexico, the guard who had intercepted the conversation got back on his cellular phone and reported every detail of the fiasco to his wife.

"From what you say, dear, I think I know who it is. When the woman I suspect crosses back into the U.S., ask passport control to detain her. If my theory is correct, it will be obvious what she is smuggling and how she's doing it." She explained her theory, leaving the guard to marvel at the brilliant woman he'd married.

The Suicidal House Guest

Doctor Paul Yancy tiptoed out of the sickroom, closing the door behind him. "Uncle Ben needs peace and quiet," he told his brother and sister-in-law. "The flu has left him weak and depressed. But the old man should make a full recovery."

"Thank goodness," replied Fritz with as much sincerity as he could muster. Uncle Ben had been staying with them ever since he got sick two weeks earlier. Every day Fritz had to remind himself of the 30 million good reasons why he and Caroline had to be hospitable to the cantankerous old man.

"Call me if he gets worse," Paul said as he left the house.

"Why can't Paul take Uncle Ben in?" Caroline whined, not for the first time.

"Very simple," Fritz explained again. "The nicer we are to the old buzzard, the more he'll leave us in his will."

A minute later, they heard the television go on

in their uncle's ground-floor room. "At least when he's watching T.V., he's not making demands," Caroline sighed.

They listened as Uncle Ben channel-surfed for a few minutes, then switched off the set. An hour later, Caroline brought in his lunch on a tray. That's when they found Uncle Ben dead, a half-empty glass of water on his nightstand along with a completely empty bottle of liquid sleeping drops.

As the body was removed, Officer Warren inspected the room. It seemed to have every convenience for a bedridden man. He counted all the electronic or battery-operated devices: the T.V. set mounted in a ceiling corner, the radio/CD player within easy reach, the portable phone, the remote control for the blinds, an intercom, and, last but not least, the remote control to adjust the adjustable bed.

"According to the medical examiner, the overdose killed him in just a few minutes," a rookie officer informed his superior. "Since the bedroom window was locked from the inside and no one was seen entering the room, I think we can call this a definite suicide."

"Definite murder," Officer Warren countered.

What was it about the room that made Warren suspect murder? And whom did he suspect?

Solution on page 339

Looking for a Lookout

On a January night, one of the coldest of the new year, a foot patrolman was making his rounds of the downtown storefronts when a hissing cat ran past him into a nearby alley. Officer Greeley glanced after it, and the beam of a roaming flashlight caught his eye. It was coming from inside the alley window of Collins' Jewelry.

Greeley called for backup and a patrol car quickly arrived. With their guns drawn, the three officers covered the front and back exits. But it was already too late. The burglars were gone. A half-full display case made it obvious that the thieves had been alerted to the police presence.

"They must have had a lookout," Greeley said. Seconds later, his deduction was confirmed. A walkie-talkie lay on the jewelry store floor, right where the burglars had dropped it. "Quick," Greeley said. "I saw three guys loitering around. One of them has to be the lookout. If we hurry . . ."

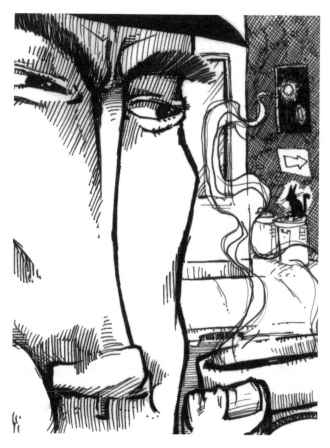

The officers did hurry. They spread out over a ten-block radius of the deserted downtown and brought in three loiterers. Greeley remembered each one.

"I was waiting for a bus," the man with the white cane and dark glasses told them. "I'm blind. I work as an accountant next door to Collins' Jewelry. Tonight I stayed late working on taxes. I heard the usual street noise, but I obviously didn't see a thing."

The second was female. "My car broke down," she said, shivering in the frigid night air. "I got out to see where exactly I was. Then I called a garage on my cell phone. You can check my car. It still won't start."

The third was a homeless alcoholic. He clutched a half-empty bottle of bourbon, the contents beginning to crystallize from the sub-freezing temperature. "I was just minding my own business," he slurred. "Trying to find someplace warm to sleep."

"A drunk, a blind man, and a stranded motorist," Greeley whispered to his colleagues. "It's pretty clear who played lookout for the burglars."

Whodunit?

Solution on page 325

High-Rise Homicide

Helen Blain said good afternoon to Morty the doorman as she walked into the lobby and took the elevator up to her fifth-floor apartment. The time was 3:55.

At 4 P.M. sharp Morty's telephone rang. "Help," a man's voice gurgled. "Stabbed. 503." Then the weak voice fell silent. Apartment 503. That was Xavier Kuralt, the Lithuanian businessman.

Morty dialed 911, then hung up and waited. Seconds later, the tenant from 505 entered the building. "What's the matter?" Alex Torful asked the visibly shaken doorman. Before Morty could answer, a siren's wail announced the approach of a squad car.

The police found the body of Xavier Kuralt on his white living-room rug, the handle of a knife protruding from his chest. "A stab wound," the senior officer said as he stepped around the single, isolated pool of blood, the only stain to mar the

pristine carpet. "It must have cut an artery. I'll bet some blood got on the killer, too."

The junior officer moved in for a closer look and nearly tripped over a long telephone cord. The receiver was still in the dead man's hand while the phone itself sat on a desk 15 feet away. The doorman was the first name listed on the telephone's speed dial. "After the assailant left, the dying man must have staggered to the phone and pressed #1," the junior officer said.

"The building has a fire exit," Morty volunteered. "The killer could've left that way—without me seeing him." But the police didn't have to look outside the building to find suspects.

Helen Blain was Xavier's next-door neighbor and his girlfriend. When the police knocked on her door, she was just coming out of the shower. "I got home a few minutes before four," she testified. "I knocked on Xavier's door, just for a chat. He didn't seem to be in."

Axel Torful was the victim's other neighbor and his business partner. As far as the police could determine, these were the foreigner's only friends and the only two with possible motives.

The Coach's Last Play

Juliet Bricker watched as her husband dawdled over his Saturday morning breakfast. "What's wrong, dear?"

Coach Bricker could never hide anything from Juliet. "It's one of my star players. I found out the boy's involved with gamblers. Maybe he's not trying to throw games, but it's still enough to get him suspended and ruin his chances with the pros."

Juliet was sympathetic. College football was his whole life, and for the first time in years, Halberton State had a great team. "What are you going to do?"

"We're meeting at the field before practice. I have to hear his side of it."

Bricker kissed his wife good-bye, picked up his latest paperback novel, and headed for the door. Bricker was always reading—a holdover from his days as an English professor.

The team coordinator showed up half an hour before practice and found the coach lying in the middle of the field, his head bashed in.

"He didn't die instantly," the police chief said as he examined the scene. A ten-foot-long blood trail showed that Bricker had been crawling toward the fieldhouse. "What's this in his hand?" The chief peered in the clenched fist and saw the last page of Coach Bricker's paperback. The rest of the book lay back at the scene of the attack.

The Halberton team had three star players and these three became immediate suspects.

"I was in my dorm room all morning," said quarterback Matt McGuffin. "Coach said I had to spend some time reviewing the playbook."

On hearing the news, Alfie Goodall, defensive lineman, broke down and could barely blubber out his alibi. "Coach told me I had to lose some weight. I was out on the road this morning, running."

Donny Emory, tight end, claimed to be sleeping in. "Me and my roommate had a late night. He's still fast asleep. I barely got here in time for practice."

The chief thought over the case until it dawned on him. "Holy cow! Before he died, Coach Bricker identified his killer. Very clever."

Whom does the chief suspect?

Solution on page 308

Long-Distance Murder

Nurse Abbott had just received her regular 10 P.M. call from Melba, the daughter-in-law of her patient, multimillionaire John Cord. As usual, Nurse Abbott put the irritating woman on the speakerphone as she tried to straighten up the kitchen. "Yes, I gave him his 9:30 medication," Nurse Abbott sighed. "Yes, he's in the study, having his tea. Is there anything else?" These conversations could go on for hours.

"Jimmy!" the nurse heard Melba shout to her husband. The annoying voice bellowed through the speakerphone. "Pick up the extension. Didn't you have a question for Nurse Abbott?"

The nurse sighed again. "Hello, Mr. Cord." She answered a few more useless questions from John Cord's son, then tactfully found a way to hang up.

Nurse Abbott finished her chore and then returned to the study. That's when she found the body of John Cord lying crumpled on the

53

Oriental carpet. A breeze from the open French doors played through a scarf that was wrapped tightly around his neck.

The police combed the crime scene and found no clue to the killer's identity. Even the study's extension phone had been wiped clean of prints. "When did you last see the deceased?" asked the homicide captain.

"About 9:45," said Nurse Abbott. "I brought him his tea in the study. He was on the phone to his lawyer. Mr. Cord was always fiddling with his will. It got to the point where we no longer paid attention. I went to the kitchen to straighten up and wait for his daughter-in-law's call. It was just like any other evening."

"Not quite," said the captain. He was examining the phone records that had just arrived via fax. "Mrs. Cord telephoned from her home 30 miles away?"

"Yes. So it had to be an intruder," Nurse Abbott theorized. "Maybe a burglar or a hired assassin. Mr. Cord had his share of business enemies."

"No. I think it was someone a lot closer to home."

Whom did the captain suspect and why?

Solution on page 324

The Queen Glendora Photos

"Your regular two o'clock appointment is here," came the secretary's voice over the intercom.

Alicia Bonwit looked up from her cluttered desk. "What? Is it Wednesday already? I don't have time." Then she got a glimpse of her frazzled hair in the mirror. "Well, perhaps I'll make time. Send them in."

The team trooped into the editor's office— Fernando, a blond, clean-shaven hair stylist; Dodo, a tall, red-headed manicurist; and Mr. Mark, a distinguished, gray-bearded dress designer. Alicia pushed aside the stacks of work. "What a day!" she exclaimed with a sigh and delivered herself into their care.

"I've been so busy, I haven't even looked at the Queen Glendora photos." Alicia pointed to an unopened, padded envelope sitting among the editorial debris. "The paparazzi have been working overtime trying to catch a shot of the Albanian queen and her secret lover. Other magazines would pay a fortune for such pictures, but I got 'em. And I haven't had a free second to open the envelope. Oh, well, first things first. What are we going to do with my hair?"

For the next hour, the editor-in-chief of the fashionable tabloid *Scoop Weekly* allowed herself to be pampered. She gossiped, looked at fabric samples, and watched as her hair and nails were returned to their usual luster. It was only after the entourage had left that she noticed the missing envelope. "The Glendora photos," Alicia shrieked and immediately rang Security.

In the main lobby's trash can, right by the men's room door, a guard found the empty envelope, the reinforced paper neatly cut in a short, scalloped pattern. A week later, the pictures popped up in *True Gossip Monthly*.

"I had no idea they were stolen," the *TGM* publisher said with a shrug. "The photos were brought to us by a man wearing dark glasses, a fake beard, and a wig. Not unusual for us. We

paid half a million in cash."

The police followed their one solid lead and quickly captured the thief.

What was the lead and who was the thief?

Solution on page 335

The Dirty Cop

For six months, a dirty cop had been leaking information to the mob, and Officer Bill Brady of Internal Affairs was going to catch him tonight. According to Brady's sources, Carmine Catrone, a mob boss, was scheduled to meet the dirty cop in Hannibal's, an out-of-the-way tavern.

Brady arrived at Hannibal's wearing a wig and false mustache. A familiar face was already on the premises—Marjorie Pepper, a desk sergeant from the Fourth Precinct. Brady watched as Marjorie ordered a drink, then lifted her left arm and checked her watch. Was she waiting for someone?

Seconds later, another familiar face entered, this time from the direction of the rest rooms. It was Adam Paprika of the Special Vice unit. As Adam used his right hand to zip up his trousers, Brady noticed the diamond pinkie ring. It reminded him of Carmine Catrone's pinkie ring.

Then came a third familiar face. Rookie patrolman Charlie Salt walked in and ambled over to an empty table. Charlie opened his briefcase and began writing down notes. When the young officer lifted his left hand to call over the waitress, Brady saw the glint of a gold fountain pen. Very expensive.

Brady had never counted on more than one officer showing up. What if they recognized each other? What if they recognized him?

As the bar grew crowded, Brady kept an eye on his subjects. All three were smoking. And all three occasionally got up to use the phone or buy cigarettes or use the rest rooms.

At the end of an hour, the suspects had all left, each one alone. Carmine Catrone had never shown up.

A frustrated Brady wandered past the pay phone. That's when he saw the matchbook in the wastebasket. On a hunch, Brady retrieved it, opening the flap. Four matches had been torn from the left side, and on the top flap was scrawled a phone number—Carmine Catrone's phone number.

Brady reasoned it out. One of his suspects had

phoned Catrone, warning him not to come. And Brady knew just who it was.

Who was it? And how did Brady know?

Solution on page 312

The Stolen Cleopatra

The silent alarm announced a break-in at the home of Jordan Marsh, the famous collector. When a patrolman arrived, he found two men waiting for him in the backyard of Marsh's suburban home, standing by a broken window.

"My name's Digby Dunne," the first man said. "Jordan's next-door neighbor. I caught this man red-handed, breaking in and stealing the Cleopatra coin."

"I caught him red-handed," the other man countered. "I'm Kenny Johnson, Jordan's other neighbor."

"One at a time," the patrolman said. "Mr. Dunne?"

"Jordan's been away for a month," Digby explained. "He gave me house keys and the alarm code. Every five days, I go in to water the plants. I was just about to do that this afternoon. I was in the process of unlocking Jordan's front door when

I looked in. Kenny was in the living room, taking a small plastic frame from the display cabinet. It was Jordan's prized Cleopatra coin. Kenny saw me and rushed out into the kitchen. I raced around the house and caught up with him in the backyard."

"That's a lie," Kenny said. "I was in my second-floor office. When I heard the sound of breaking glass, I looked out. Digby was in Jordan's yard, by the kitchen door. He must have just broken a windowpane. In his hand I could see the plastic holder for the Cleopatra coin. I raced downstairs and surprised him before he could leave the yard. He must have gotten in with his key, stolen the coin, then faked the break-in to throw off suspicion."

The patrolman entered Jordan Marsh's house and found an empty spot in the display cabinet. By the doorway of the sunlit kitchen, he examined a potted plant. The soil was dry and the lush, long leaves were bent toward the darkened living room. Re-emerging into the yard, he found the morning rain had left muddy patches. Rows of brown footprints trailed across the flagstones.

Both men insisted on being searched, but the

65

patrolman refused. "I don't need to search anyone. I know which one of you is lying."

Whodunit? And where is the coin hidden?

Solution on page 337

Archie's Christmas Surprise

"Mr. Granger?" The secretary tried to speak calmly into the receiver. "This is Emily. Could you come down to the nineteenth floor? It's sort of an emergency."

Emily hung up. It was an emergency, all right. Archie Tatum, their chief financial officer, was in his office, hanging by a rope from an extremely strong light fixture. He had been like this when Hank, his assistant, came to work. Hank was used to seeing him in the office before anyone else, but not like this. Hank had waited for Emily to arrive. She'd know what to do.

Emily's reaction had been cool. "What a horrible thing—and on the last work day before Christmas! Call the police. I'll get Mr. Granger down here."

From the moment Gene Granger stepped out

of the elevator, he was enmeshed in damage control. As president of Granger Productions, he had to break the news to the rest of the company and then deal with the press, the police, and Archie's family.

Granger didn't even think about returning to the twentieth floor until Emily reminded him at 5 P.M. "The Christmas party upstairs, Mr. Granger. People won't stay long, but I think everyone could use a little comfort."

Several employees were already gathered as Granger unlocked the door of his private conference room. A Christmas tree was in the corner, with a colorful jumble of presents under its branches. Emily crossed to the bar and immediately began serving. Despite the alcohol, the mood remained somber. Granger handed out a personally chosen gift to each worker, from the secretaries to the executive vice-president.

Hank was one of the last to leave. He took one final look at the empty floor under the tree, then turned to join his fiancée.

"What could have driven Archie to suicide?" his fiancée wondered. "Emily says he'd been very

69

worried about company finances. You don't suppose that maybe he was embezzling . . ."

"Archie didn't kill himself," Hank responded. He was murdered. And I know who did it."

Whodunit? And how did Hank know?

Solution on page 303

Postgraduate Murder

The time of death was firmly established. At 10:06 P.M. all three suspects said they heard a gunshot echo through the house. The house was shared by four graduate students; three, if you no longer counted Harry Harris, the victim who lay in his second-story bedroom, a bullet in his chest.

Harry, it seemed, had been a ladies' man. He had even bragged about seducing the girlfriend of one of his housemates. Unfortunately, the police didn't know which one. They separated the three remaining housemates and interviewed each one.

"I was working on my car," Bill Mayer insisted. "I plugged an extension cord into an outlet behind the house. Then I took a work light around to the side driveway, in front of the garage. When I heard the gunshot, it took me a second to realize it came from the house. Then I ran inside."

The second suspect entered the room with a noticeable limp. "I had just come home," explained Sonny Sorriso. "I parked in the alley behind the house. I was walking up to the back door when I tripped hard over some cord. I fell down, then just sat there, nursing my ankle. Maybe two minutes later came the gunshot. That got me moving."

The third suspect claimed that he had just come down to the kitchen. "I was starting to scoop out a bowl of ice cream," said Glen Gouly. "Then I heard a noise out back. I looked out, but it was dark. I went back to my ice cream. A couple minutes later I heard the shot."

The detectives circled the house. In the kitchen, they found a melted bowl of ice cream on the counter by the refrigerator. In the backyard, they saw an orange extension cord with a bent prong that had been ripped from an outdoor socket. Following the extension cord around, they found Bill Mayer's car in front of the garage, the work light suspended over the open hood.

"It's pretty clear who's lying," the chief detective mumbled.

Whodunit?

Solution on page 331

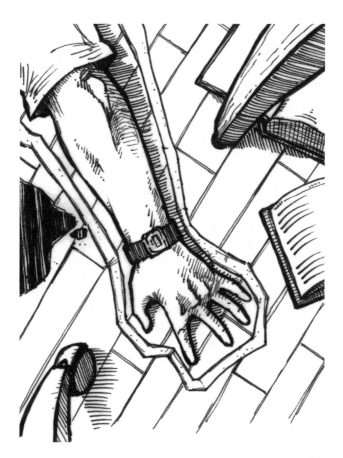

The Last Poker Hand

A homicide sergeant stood in the hotel suite, gazing down at the body of Bugsy Ferret. "He was a card sharp," the sergeant told the hotel manager. "Bugsy preyed on tourists. He'd lure them to a hotel, start a friendly poker game, and take them to the cleaners. I guess someone came back this time and took Bugsy."

Bugsy lay sprawled amid a carpet of scattered playing cards and a bottle of Blush gin. He'd been stabbed in the chest.

"Looks like he didn't die right away," said the sergeant as he pointed to the five cards held in the victim's stiff grip. All diamonds. "Maybe he was trying to tell us something."

"We got our suspects," came a voice from the bedroom. The sergeant's partner emerged, holding a handwritten list. "Benny King, Jack Lawrence, Joe Blush, Alan Spade. He listed their hotels, too. Let's check 'em out."

The Reverend Benny King denied knowing Bugsy and vehemently denied ever playing poker. "My parishioners know I would never risk their money—or mine—in such a sinful pursuit. I don't know how my name got on that list."

Jack Lawrence told a different story. "Sure, King was there. And Al Spade and Joe Flush. The four of us first met yesterday at a hotel bar. We got to talking about cards and this Ferret character talked us into a game. Hey, you live and learn."

Alan Spade was a tad more sanguine. "He was a stinking cheat and he deserved to die. I was livid, but we all paid up and we left the rat in one piece. Someone must've come back, but it wasn't me."

Joseph Blush, an English professor, seemed an unlikely gambler. "At first we all won our share. But as the evening progressed, we lost more. I don't suppose you can give me my money back." The police assured him that no money had been found in Bugsy Ferret's suite.

"We should bring one of them in for questioning," the sergeant said after the final interview.

Which card player did he suspect?

Solution on page 323

The Pretenders' Ball

The secret police warned the prime minister to cancel the Pretenders' Ball. But the costume ball was a 200-year-old tradition in the small Grand Duchy. Despite threats from the rebels, the annual celebration had to take place as scheduled.

The prime minister made a handful of concessions to security. The peg-legged pirate had his sword confiscated, and the Turkish sultan gave up his curved, bulky dagger. But the baseball player was allowed to keep his bat, and the chukka sticks were not taken from the masked Ninja. No one was expecting an attack by a blunt instrument.

But that's exactly what happened. On one of the palace's two dozen balconies, the 80-year-old grand duke was cornered by an assassin and bludgeoned to death. When the chief of police discovered the body, the old duke, dressed as a peasant, was draped over a ledge, his royal blood dripping into the dark chasm below.

"Quick," the chief said to the nearest costumed reveler. "Close the doors. Alert the guards."

The pirate, in reality a provincial mayor, immediately ran to obey, taking the steps two at a time down to the main ballroom.

"We have to find the murder weapon," the chief's assistant said a few minutes later as he lined up all the shocked and grief-stricken guests.

The baseball player, the prime minister's political rival, said he might have left his bat upstairs. An aide went in search and found it in a spittoon just outside the men's bathroom.

The masked Ninja, they were surprised to discover, was the prime minister's own niece, one of the duchy's only feminists. Her chukka sticks, which had originally been on her belt, were now in a deep side pocket of her black robes. "They got in the way when I danced," she explained.

"Take everything," the chief barked. "The American Embassy will do chemical tests for us. We'll find the cowardly assassin."

"We don't need tests," whispered the prime minister, speaking for the first time since the murder. "I know who killed the duke and what the weapon was."

Whodunit?

Solution on page 332

Good-Neighbor Policy

"I was trying to be a good neighbor," Jake Spado told the sergeant. "I was watching T.V. at about midnight when Shamus started barking next door. The Whitakers were away. So out I went in the driving rain. I made a circuit of the Whitaker house. Everything seemed safe and secure, so I went back home." Jake bristled. "And here's the thanks I get, being suspected of burglary."

The other neighbor told a slightly different story. Millie Overlock had been awakened by the barking. "I finally got up and looked out. By the light of a street lamp I could see Jake disappear around the side of the Whitaker house. A few minutes later he came around the other side, then went back toward his own house. Since I was up, I made myself a cup of tea. The rain was just stopping as I got back into bed." Millie leaned over to the sergeant. "It had to be Jake. Shamus barks when anyone comes near, even the Whitakers. I would have heard if Shamus had started up again."

The sergeant went from Millie's to the crime scene. As expected, the rottweiler let out a chorus of barks. Jimmy, the Whitakers' nephew, quieted Shamus, then invited the officer in to inspect the damage in the rear living area.

"When I came by this morning to walk Shamus, I found it like this." He pointed to an open window and the broken pane of glass just above the window latch. "Shamus has a killer bark, but he wouldn't hurt a fly. The thief obviously knew this. He also knew about the diamond earrings my aunt just bought. They were in the Chinese box on the mantel."

The sergeant knelt down under the open window. The fluffy carpet was marred only by broken shards of glass and a series of muddy footprints leading to and from the mantel. "Those shoe prints could be a clue," Jimmy suggested.

"I have all the clues I need," the sergeant replied confidently.

What had the sergeant deduced?

Solution on page 317

Killer Camp Food

The Tafel nephews had finally persuaded their sedentary Uncle Gil to go camping with them. "I love food and I hate discomfort," the heavyset man protested as he wedged his huge frame into the four-wheel drive. "This will be the death of me."

On the first evening it poured. The nephews all pitched in, building a fire and setting up a rain cover for food preparation. The ensuing meal was haphazard, with each camper fixing a plate for himself, then scurrying back to his own tent and eating alone.

As they finished their meal, the rain stopped. Ed, the eldest, was the first one out of his tent. "I hope Uncle Gil got enough to eat," he said as he surveyed the empty pots.

His youngest brother joined him under the dripping tarp. "You can bet on it," Richie said, flashing his usual, dazzling white smile. "I saw

him going back for thirds."

The middle brother, Pete, was the last one out. They washed the pots in the river, then, on their way back, stopped by Uncle Gil's tent. He lay collapsed among his empty plates. Dead.

"A heart attack," Pete deduced. "I mean, it couldn't have been the food. We all ate the same things."

"Not quite." Richie was eyeing the dead man's glass. "Maybe it was the wine. I don't drink white wine and Ed doesn't drink at all."

"I had some wine," Pete said, "so it couldn't have been tainted. What about the freeze-dried shrimp soup? Richie and I are both allergic to shellfish."

"I had a big bowl and it was fine," Ed volunteered. "What about the blueberry cobbler? Pete never eats dessert. And by the time I got back to sample it, it was gone. Maybe Uncle Gil ate it all."

"No," Richie said. "I had a huge portion. Between the two of us, Uncle and I finished it off."

Based on their discussion, the brothers dismissed the idea of food poisoning. But two days later, at the autopsy, potassium cyanide was found in the old millionaire's system.

One of the nephews was obviously lying. Which one?

Solution on page 322

Eye Spy

The American agent used his skeleton keys to work on the lock while his female partner acted as lookout. It was hard to see clearly in the dreary hall light in the dreary apartment building in the dreary winter weather of Beijing. But David Richman finally cracked the mechanism and opened the door. "Hurry," he whispered, motioning for Julia to join him. Inside it was just as chilly as the hall.

"We're looking for photographic negatives," he told Julia for perhaps the tenth time. "35 millimeter. Lu Ching hasn't had time to reduce them any further. Thank goodness it's a small apartment."

It was small, all right. The tiny studio contained a futon bed that doubled as a sofa. There were also a bookcase, a table, two chairs, and an old-fashioned desk fan that whirred noisily on top of a cluttered desk. A hot plate served as the apartment's kitchen. From a small adjoining bathroom

came the sound of a leaky toilet.

"We have to find them," David whispered as he went directly for the bookcase. "The lives of a dozen Chinese contacts depend on our finding those eight negatives." He was already going through the books page by page, checking the covers for any telltale slits where the agent for the People's Republic might have stuffed them.

"Lu Ching didn't have a lot of time to hide them," David added. "And he needed to keep them in a pretty accessible place. It shouldn't be too hard."

But it was. They checked under everything, from the desk clutter to the chair seats. They checked the water flow in all the faucets and the toilet tank. David became so frustrated he was almost ready to cut open the futon.

Julia stepped back and surveyed the room. "I see it now. I know where they probably are," she said softly.

What clue is Julia looking at?

Solution on page 314

The Piney Bluffers

"I was just pulling into the Piney Bluffs gas station," the shaken witness told the operator. "I heard a gunshot. And then I saw the men—two of them—running out of the station and hopping into a recreation vehicle. They'd killed the attendant." She gave a description of the R.V. and a general description of the men.

The R.V. was found, abandoned south of one of the roadblocks the highway patrol had set up. The vehicle was just feet away from Piney Bluffs State Park, which was enjoying its first rain in weeks. It was assumed that the men had hiked away into the hundreds of acres of park land. Officers were sent in to interview the campers.

"Sorry we can't help you," Warren Hatchet told an officer. He and his brother were camping in a tent by a trout stream. They fit the general description. "We hiked in here last night. All day today we've been fishing. Got back just a little while ago."

"You fished in the rain?" the officer asked as he gazed at the two small trout frying in a pan. The brothers invited him to join them for dinner, but he refused.

A second pair of campers also fit the description. The officer joined them inside their tent, sitting on a knapsack in order to avoid the wet ground. "This morning we set up camp," Al Fishburn told him. "Then we went out hiking. When it started raining, we found a cave and holed up there for a few hours. We didn't see anyone—not until you came along."

A final pair of campers were discovered in an R.V. in a section of the park off-limits to vehicles. "I know we shouldn't be here," George Tingle said. "But we're not hurting anyone. A friend in Chicago lent me this R.V. That's why the registration's not in my name. If you want to call Chicago and check . . ."

"I don't need to call anyone," the officer replied. "I already know who's lying."

Whodunit? And how did the officer know?

Solution on page 330

The Vandalizing Visitor

It was late at night at the Drakemore Hotel. A member of the cleaning staff was dusting the courtesy phones in the lobby when she heard the breaking of glass in the side lobby. And then the alarm went off.

The side lobby contained a display case holding memorabilia from the Drakemore's opening fifty years ago: the hotel's first menu, a laughably antiquated price list for rooms, a few rare coins and stamps from that year, photographs, and the dusty signatures of the first famous guests.

The night manager showed up a few seconds later. He and the staff member circled the lobby and discovered three guests who had been in the vicinity. Diplomatically but firmly, the manager suggested all three remain in the lobby until the police arrived.

"We've had them under constant observation," the manager told the responding officer. He

pointed to a woman reading in an armchair. "Ms. Oakley said she had just returned from a business dinner. She was very cooperative. Just sat down and pulled a book out of her briefcase."

"Mr. Brier said he'd come down from his room to get some aspirin from the front desk. His wife had a headache. When we detained him, he called his wife on one of the pay phones. I listened in. He told her he would be delayed and not to worry."

The manager pointed to the last suspect, a sloppily dressed young man who looked like he'd had one too many. "Mr. Greenleaf had been in the hotel bar. The bartender refused to serve him any more alcohol, so he wandered in here. We found him by the elevator, jamming his finger into the 'up' button."

"Whoever did this wasn't counting on an alarm," the manager continued. "Perhaps he was scared off before he took anything. We may never know who tried to rob us."

"I have a good idea who it was," the officer said. "One of the suspects did something odd. Just let me have one thing checked."

An Attack of Gas

The island of Canary Rock had no police force and none was really needed—not until the fateful morning when Gerald Espy was found dead in his bed. The millionaire had been laid up with a broken leg, and although the local doctor was adept at setting bones, he was not well versed in murder. It wasn't until he saw the dead cat curled up in a corner that he even suspected foul play.

"Poison gas," the inspector guessed when he arrived. An empty glass container on the table was the primary evidence. "Pour one chemical on another." He pointed to the dead flies on the windowsill at the east end of the room. "In less than a minute everything in the room would be dead."

The body had been discovered by Espy's son, Melvin. "I was out with some friends on my boat. I dropped them off at about midnight, then motored back to Canary Rock. There were no lights on at the house, but every now and then the

moon would peek through. I figured Dad was asleep. So I locked up the house and went straight to bed. This morning, I went to check up. He was dead."

The last person to admit seeing Gerald Espy alive was his business partner, Frank Townly, another island resident. "Frank came in here around midnight," the tavern owner testified. "He and Espy weren't getting along. Business was bad and they were both threatening lawsuits. Frank drank down a slew of scotches. He told me he had just been over to Espy's. When it came closing time, Frank was dead drunk and asleep. I just locked up and left him in there. He was still asleep at noontime when I opened up."

"When I left Gerald's house last night, he was alive," the hung-over Frank Townly said. "Check the time of death."

"I don't have to check the time of death," the inspector replied. "I have a pretty good idea when it was done and who did it."

Or, as we like to say: whodunit?

Solution on page 304

An Inside Job

The schedule at Klein Miller Accounting ran like clockwork. For example, on Friday mornings, Arthur Klein always took the train from their Connecticut offices into Manhattan. He would return at 1 P.M. and go immediately into the partners' meeting. Except for this Friday. On this Friday, he was mugged and robbed seconds after arriving in Manhattan.

The New York police held out little hope. "It was just bad luck," a sergeant commiserated. "There's no way a mugger could know you were carrying those bearer bonds."

"I normally don't carry anything," Klein moaned. "But one of our clients needed to transport the bonds to his New York bank. I agreed to take them—as a favor. This will ruin us."

The next train to Connecticut was at 1:10 and Klein was on it. Immediately on arriving, he met with Phil Miller, the other senior partner. "I didn't

tell the police this," Arthur confided. "But some-one here must have been in on the theft. The mugger was following me. He knew I had the bonds."

The two partners walked past the conference room where Betty, their executive assistant, had just finished setting up for the partners' meeting. "That's quite an accusation," Phil whispered.

The third partner, Melinda Crowley, waved at Klein from her office. "About time you showed up. I have things to discuss at the meeting—including my resignation," she added with a grin. "I'm getting married and moving to New York." Klein and Miller had heard endless tales about Melinda's rich and devoted boyfriend. Apparently, the stories were true.

The fourth partner was Vern Underwood, just a month away from mandatory retirement. When informed of the theft during the meeting, Vern was livid. "This is a plot. The three of you faked the robbery. You're trying to lower the firm's value, just when I'm being forced to cash in. I'll sue."

Arthur Klein gazed down the long meeting table, at the carafes of water and the carefully coded folders of old and new business. And suddenly he knew.

What did Klein know? Whodunit?

Solution on page 320

The Convent Mystery

"We have a little mystery at the Inner City Convent," the Mother Superior said as she poured a second cup of tea.

Inspector Griffith was immediately interested.

"It's the convent offices. We have three civilian employees there to handle the mail and the bills and the bookkeeping. Alice has been with us for years. Very reliable, even though she has a bit of a drinking problem and a husband who . . . Let's just say he can use our prayers.

"Barbara is new. She worked at an Alaskan convent before coming here. She's seems wonderful, although we're still waiting for the sisters there to send us a character reference.

"Our third is Claudia. Ever since the city opened up riverboat gambling . . . Well, I'm not going to point fingers, but there have been some minor irregularities in our petty cash.

"As you know, the office is closed all weekend.

On Monday morning I arrive first. I open up, check the mail, water the plants, turn off the alarm. We have this newfangled alarm system. It does all the usual. And it also automatically records whenever the alarm has been turned off. I never quite saw the sense of that. But four Mondays ago when I came in, I checked the log. The alarm had been turned off Saturday afternoon. For five minutes. Then it was switched back on. I didn't think anything of it. Someone probably came back to retrieve some forgotten item.

"The next Monday, I found the same thing. Turned off Saturday afternoon for five minutes. I asked the women—they all have alarm keys. All three denied having visited the office.

"This has been going on for four Saturdays now. Nothing is ever missing or changed. Even the petty cash is exactly the same as it was Friday evening. It's baffling—although I don't suppose there's any harm done."

"There could be harm," Inspector Griffith replied. "I can think of only one possible explanation. And I think we need to deal with this woman right away."

Death by Chocolate

The four finalists lined up in the hotel ballroom, all smiling for the photographers and all wearing knee-length aprons, each custom-made apron proclaiming "The Great Dessert Bake-Off." Bob Bullock's smile was genuine. His entry, "Death by Chocolate," had been a runaway favorite in the preliminaries. And the others knew it.

"I'm going up to my room for a nap," the lanky Texan drawled as he folded his apron and tucked it under his arm. "See you gals at the finals."

One of the the three "gals" smiled back with a murderous gleam. "Not if I can help it." She waited five minutes, then wiped her sweaty palms on her apron and headed for the elevator.

An hour later, a maid found the body. Bob Bullock was laid out on his bed, still dressed in his cowboy shirt and jeans, his head smashed in by a cooking mallet. Blood was splattered everywhere.

The police ruled out robbery. The chef's wallet

111

had been untouched. And all of his clothes—two shirts, two pairs of jeans, socks, shoes, underwear, jacket, and a tall chef's toque—seemed to be present and accounted for.

When the police knocked on Vanna Blackhorn's door, they had to wait. "I was in the shower," she explained as she began toweling off her short black hair. "I came back here straight from the photo session. I want to look my best when I win tonight."

They found the second finalist also in her room. Dotty Minton invited them in, then went back to washing out a sweater in the sink. "I should've known better than to wear a long-sleeved sweater when I cook. I don't think this strawberry stain will ever come out."

The police didn't get to Kelly Yeagar until just before the finals. She was already dressed to go, wearing her best blouse and skirt, covered by a bake-off apron. "I'm ready," she told the coordinator and didn't even notice the detective. "If I'm not going to win, I might as well look good," she joked, then bent over to straighten the apron that was bunching up around her calves.

The detective introduced himself, and then, for the third time, explained about Bob Bullock's murder. "You don't have to worry, Ms. Yeagar. Everything's under control. We know who killed him."

Whodunit? And how did they know?

Solution on page 310

A Quali-Tee Theft

"I can't give you anything for this. It's junk." Abe Ketchum pushed the watch back across the counter. The Quali-Tee Pawn Shop was a class establishment and, as the manager, Abe had to maintain certain standards. The would-be customer, a shabby young man who smelled of liquor, took back the worthless item and shuffled dejectedly out onto the street, lingering in front of the windows to inspect the shiny display of abandoned valuables.

Abe's assistant bustled out from the back room. "I'm leaving," Mark said. That was nothing unusual. Mark Price was the owner's nephew and was always either coming in late or leaving early. Abe felt particularly overworked and under-appreciated as he watched his privileged assistant breeze out the door.

Abe had one more customer that day. A well-dressed woman walked in and timidly offered an

emerald brooch. Abe instantly recognized the quality of the piece and offered her as much as he was permitted. He was surprised when she accepted. Like many of his customers, she seemed desperate.

That night, a burglar alarm echoed through the neighborhood. The police arrived just a few minutes later, but the deed was already done. A thief had broken a display window, jumped inside the crowded shop, and left with many of the most valuable items.

"He was a quick one," an officer said to Abe with begrudging admiration. "Half a dozen rings from the jewelry case, some rare coins that didn't even have price tags on. He even broke the lock on the bottom drawer of your file cabinet. What was in there?"

"Loose diamonds," Abe sighed. "Let me check something."

Abe crossed to the cash register. It was open and empty, but when he pulled the drawer out all the way, he saw a flash of light. "Aha! Something our thief missed." And he pulled out the emerald brooch. "I didn't have time to put it in a display case. I guess that's what saved it."

Within a week the police had tracked down some of the stolen items and made an arrest.
Whodunit?

Solution on page 334

The Three Stoogles

When the police arrived at Hubert Stoogle's house, the motif seemed to be water. The sprinkler system was going full force, and the owner of the premises was lying dead in his own bathtub.

The man's three nephews lined up on the sun-drenched front porch, each one eager to tell his story.

"Once a week Uncle Hubert had us over for lunch," Stanley Stoogle said. "I parked in the front drive. Uncle wasn't around, so I assumed he was taking his usual soak. As I went into the library, a summer shower passed over. Five minutes later, the sun was out again. It was a few minutes after that when I heard Uncle shouting. Then all the lights sputtered and went out. I went upstairs and found him. Someone had thrown an electric hair dryer into his tub."

"I got here during the shower," volunteered

Dick Stoogle. His hair and clothes were still wet. "I parked behind Stanley. Just running up to the porch I got drenched. I was in a downstairs bathroom drying off when I heard the shout and saw the lights go off. When I got up to Uncle's bathroom, Stanley was standing over the tub. A wet hair dyer was in his hand."

Eugene said he arrived last. "The shower was long over. The driveway was full of cars, so I parked by the rear garden. Once inside, I noticed the place was dark. I wandered around, looking for my brothers. Then Stanley came down and told me the news."

The boys all agreed about what happened next. Eugene ran out to move his car. "The darn sprinklers had gone on and the inside of my convertible was soaked." Meanwhile, Stanley went downstairs to replace the blown fuse, and Dick used his cellular phone to call the police.

Hubert Stoogle's maid had been cooking in the kitchen and couldn't support anyone's alibi. "All of them could be telling the truth," she told an officer.

"No," the officer answer. "One of them is lying.

The Shortcut Robbery

It was 1 P.M. when the two officers heard the cry for help. They responded quickly, racing down an alley to find a woman sitting on the ground, massaging a nasty bump on the back of her head. It took them a minute to get her to speak coherently.

Her name was Mary Ramsey. She worked at a jewelry store and had been in the process of taking yesterday's receipts to the bank. "I do this every day. My boss warned me not to use the alley. Today I had a feeling I was being followed. Like an idiot, I took the alley anyway. I heard footsteps. Before I could even turn around, I was hit on the head.

"I fell down," Mary continued. "But it didn't quite knock me out. He was running away with my money bag. I only saw him from the rear. He was tall and had on blue jeans and a dark-colored cardigan."

The officers brought in two men for question-

ing, both tall and both dressed according to Mary's description.

"So, I was running," Stu Logan said angrily. He had been found two blocks from the site of the attack and ran as soon as he saw the patrol car. Stu had a string of priors, all misdemeanors "Look, I was at the end of my lunch break. I can't be late getting back to work. I need this job." Stu, it turned out, worked at the deli right next to the jewelry store.

The second suspect was Ollie Oscar, a street person. "I wasn't even wearing this sweater," he protested as he unbuttoned his moth-eaten cardigan. "I picked it out of the garbage just before you pulled me in."

"And what about this money bag?" the officer asked, pointing to the other item found on him.

"I got that from a different garbage can. The ones behind the bank always have things like this. You didn't find any money on me. Right?"

The officers agreed that there was only one suspect worth considering.

Whodunit?

Solution on page 336

The Locked Room

"I'm changing my will," Abigail Wallace announced. Her four children might have been adopted, but they were just as spoiled and ungrateful as any natural offspring. "Tomorrow I'm cutting you all off without a cent." And with that satisfying but reckless statement, Abigail rose from the dining room table and headed up to her bedroom.

No one was surprised when a gunshot rang out two hours later. The only surprise was that it had taken so long.

"I was downstairs reading," Manny later told the police. "As soon as I heard the shot, I ran upstairs and down the hall to Mother's room. It was locked from the inside."

Moe had also been downstairs, in the kitchen. "I ran up the back staircase. Manny was already at Mother's door, pounding and calling out her name."

"I was in my own room at the far end of the hall," said Jack, the third child to arrive at the scene. "I suggested looking through the keyhole. But Manny and Moe decided to put their shoulders to the door instead."

After a few tries, the doorjamb cracked open and the sons rushed in to find Abigail Wallace seated in her chair, her hand flailed limply over the armrest with the gun on the rug right below.

The boys heard a gasp and turned around to see their sister, Sheila, behind them in the doorway.

"I'd been on the third floor," she later testified. "I heard the gunshot but didn't know what it was. When I heard everyone running, I came down to the second floor. They were gathered at Mother's door. Jack was looking through the keyhole. Manny and Moe shooed him away and started ramming the door. I just stood there. Only after they busted the door open did I come out of my daze and follow them in."

Faced with a locked room, the police were all prepared to call it suicide, until they heard about the will. Then they reviewed the evidence and arrested a suspect.

A Timely Alibi

The murder occurred in the wee hours of the morning on the last Sunday of October and looked like a professional hit. The victim, Sol Weintraub, ran a garbage-collection business that was going in direct competition with a mob-owned company. Days after winning a contract with the city's convention center, Sol was found dead in his suburban home.

The killer had broken into the man's house, shot him once in the head with a silencer-equipped .38, and left, taking no valuables.

It was now early November and the police were no closer to finding their killer. The medical examiner was placing the time of death at between 2 and 3 A.M. But the mob's most reliable "enforcers" all had alibis.

Johnny "Dum-Dum" Falco had been out on the town that Saturday night. Witnesses saw him at the Tropicana Club until 2 A.M. Other witnesses,

just as reliable, placed Dum-Dum at a nearby tavern from 3 A.M. until closing. No matter how the police timed it, the murder scene was a good 40 minutes away from both the Tropicana and the tavern.

Victor Conroy's alibi was even better. He'd been a patient at Mercy Memorial. The young hit man had been in a minor car accident and was being held overnight. A nurse checked his room every hour, all night. Mercy Memorial was also nearly 40 minutes from the crime.

The third suspect had been at work. A dozen coworkers placed Juan Garcia at his night job in a cement factory. He'd punched in at midnight, eaten "lunch" on the premises, and punched out Sunday morning at eight, with an hour's worth of overtime.

"The mob must have brought in someone from outside," the chief detective told his wife one evening. "Either that or we have some lying witnesses."

"Not necessarily," his wife replied. "On what date did this murder take place?" The detective told her. "Well," she said with a smile. "I can think of a way the killer could have done it. There's a hole in one of their alibis."

Whose alibi? Whodunit?

Solution on page 343

A Chinese Lie Detector

When the emperor rose on that April morning, he immediately noticed the silence. "There's no cricket. Where's my cricket?" he demanded. The servants of the bed chamber checked all the usual places, but the cricket was gone—and so was its jeweled cricket box.

The entire royal court was thrown into turmoil until the chirping pet was finally found, housed in a lowly bamboo box and hidden in the corner of a public garden. The emperor was both relieved and outraged. "How dare someone steal from me!" He ordered the captain of the palace guard to find the still-missing box and the culprit.

Finding the box was easy. Lu Ping, a near-sighted gem dealer, bought it from a palace servant and only realized later what he had purchased. With the most abject apologies, he returned it to the emperor. "I don't know if I can recognize the man who sold it to me," he said with a squint. "I'll do my best."

From the gem dealer's description, the captain narrowed down the suspects to three. But the dealer couldn't make a positive identification, and none of the three would confess. "Hang them all," the emperor commanded.

That was when the court wizard intervened. "I can discover the guilty servant," he boasted. "Bring the three and come to the public garden."

The wizard led the way to the spot where the cricket had been found. He ordered each suspect to cut a stalk of bamboo. Then the wizard planted the stalks in the hard earth, making sure that each one stuck up the same height from the ground. "By dawn tomorrow," he announced in solemn tones, "the stalk of the guilty man will grow by the length of a finger joint."

By dawn the next morning, the wizard had kept his word. He had discovered the identity of the guilty servant.

How did the wizard do it?

Solution on page 307

The Brothers Ilirium

A church choir was picnicking in a rest area near Pine Gorge when they heard the distant squeal of tires. The choir members gazed out over the winding ribbon of road in time to see a red convertible slam through a guard rail and sail out into the steep gorge. The driver was thrown clear of the vehicle seconds before impact. Miraculously, there was no explosion.

The highway patrol found the bloodied body of Mike Ilirium smashed on the boulders. Inside the mangled car were several loose rocks, a tangle of broken branches, and more blood on the seat and the dashboard.

The Ilirium saga was well known to the area gossips. Mike had been engaged to a local beauty. They broke off the engagement when she confessed to having had an affair with one of Mike's brothers; no one knew which.

The authorities visited the Ilirium lodge a half

mile up the road from the accident. Mike's two brothers seemed devastated by the news.

"Mike was in a funk," Dirk testified. "He'd been drinking all morning. Finally, he just grabbed his car keys and left. I yelled after him not to drive. I didn't hear any motor, so I thought he'd listened. Then a couple minutes later, I heard his car peel out. I would've gone after him, but there was this play-off game on T.V. I had no idea he'd kill himself."

Roger Ilirium confirmed his brother's story. "I was in the garage office, working on my computer when I heard the front door slam. I looked out the window and saw Mike stumbling around the driveway. I went back to work until I heard the ignition. I looked out again and saw Mike driving off in his convertible, weaving down the road. I wasn't too worried. Not until the highway patrol guys showed up."

The police concentrated their investigation on one of the brothers and soon had a confession.

Whodunit? What made the police suspicious?

Solution on page 305

The Pre-Valentine's Day Murder

It was the day before Valentine's Day and the police in the small college town were unprepared for any crime beyond the amorous escapades of a few undergraduates.

Late that afternoon a patrol car canvassed Oakview, a small off-campus apartment building. The officers found the body of Gilly Tarpin, a homeless drifter. He was a nondescript man of normal build, lying in the shelter of an open garage bay. The officers made an inventory of Gilly's possessions: a wristwatch (looking new, except for a vertical crease on the leather band inside the clasp), a box of chocolates (with half the contents eaten), and a crumpled pre-printed note saying "Be My Valentine."

The authorities assumed it was a natural death, caused by exposure to the February chill. But then

the mandatory autopsy came back. There was poison in the homeless man's system. An identical poison was found in the remaining candies.

The police interviewed three Oakview residents, hoping for some clue as to why anyone would poison a homeless drifter.

"I used to talk to him," said Brick Darden, the school's star fullback. "He was always hanging around, bumming cigarettes and loose change. The guy had absolutely nothing, but he was harmless."

Sawyer Prescott III had a less charitable opinion. "He was a thief," sniffed the heavyset millionaire student. "A ring disappeared from my apartment. The very next day I saw it in a pawn shop. The shop owner said he forgot who sold it to him, but I know it was that Gilly character."

Peter Peaver held the opposite opinion. "Sure he begged money," said the featherweight math major. "But Gilly was basically honest. We often forget to lock our apartments, and I never found anything missing."

"A homeless guy is poisoned with candy chocolates on the day before Valentine's Day," the homicide captain thought aloud. "I have a hunch how

A Real False Alarm

"The car alarm often goes off in hot, humid weather," Elliot Zypher told the inspector from the burglary division. "When it went off last night, I had no idea the car was actually being robbed. This has always been such a safe area."

The detective looked around at the large houses and well-tended lawns and had to agree. "Do you usually leave expensive necklaces out in the car?"

"That was my fault, inspector," answered Elliot's sister, Zelda. "I had just brought the necklace back from the jeweler. We were halfway through dinner when I remembered where it was. Neither Elliot nor I had the energy to go get it. I went right from dinner up to my room. With the windows closed and the air conditioning on, I could barely hear the horn start blaring. I assumed it was the usual false alarm."

Elliot had been downstairs when the car began its wailing. He felt just unsure enough about the

144

necklace to go out and check. "The front passenger window had been smashed in with a rock," he said. "I checked under the passenger seat. That's where I remembered Zelda placing the necklace case. But it was gone."

The only other person in the house that night had been Martha, the maid. She confirmed as much as she could of their stories, then added her own. "As I was clearing the dinner table, I thought I saw something moving out in the garden. Usually when that happens it's just my imagination. But I remembered what Ms. Zelda said about the necklace. I went out in the garden to look around. I was still there when the alarm went off. A few seconds later, I saw Mr. Elliot exit the patio doors to go check up on it."

The police dusted for prints and came up with nothing. The passenger door and seat had both been wiped clean. "I guess we're dealing with a professional," a rookie cop suggested.

"We're dealing with an inside job," his boss answered. "And I know who."

Whodunit? And how did he know?

Solution on page 335

Airport Insecurity

Phil Moretti hated it when tourists got murdered. It reflected badly on New York City, on Kennedy Airport, and especially on him, chief of airport security. Somehow it didn't seem as bad when the victim was local.

In this case it was a businessman on a flight from Chicago. He had barely gotten off the plane. At 3:42 P.M., a passerby found him stabbed to death in the men's room just a few feet from his arrival gate. The body had been robbed. No jewelry. And although the wallet and credit cards had been left behind, there was no cash.

Three suspicious characters had been seen loitering by the gates. Barely 15 minutes passed from the time of the body's discovery before all three were brought in for questioning.

The first suspect was Abe Grisham, a petty criminal with a long rap sheet. "I was just seeing off a friend," he said as he nervously twisted the

silver and onyx ring on his finger. "After her flight took off, I just hung around. I like airports."

The second was Johnny Ambrose, who had one prior arrest for grand theft auto. "I was here to pick up a friend, but his flight was canceled. I was just wasting time here till my next appointment." Johnny checked his watch. "Is this gonna take much longer? I got a 4 o'clock meeting way up in the Bronx, and I can't be late."

The last man interviewed was Doogie Weber, a suspected member of the Cordoba crime family. "One of the employees here owes me some money. I can never find the guy at home, so I tracked him down at work. That's why I got so much cash on me. I took the guy to an ATM and he gave me a payment on his debt."

Security Chief Moretti listened to all three stories, then pointed to one of the suspects. "This one we need to question further. The other two can go."

Whom did Moretti suspect and why?

Solution on page 301

The Pretenders' Ball, II

Last year's Pretenders' Ball had ended in the tragic assassination of the grand duke. Despite that disaster, the prime minister insisted on going ahead with this year's festivities. One new concession was made to security. The ball would be held during the day, giving the secret police a clearer view of the proceedings.

A bright, sunny sky greeted the costumed revelers. As usual, they were searched. The rubber daggers piercing Julius Caesar's toga were allowed in, but only after a long argument. The cowboy handed over his plastic six-shooter but got to keep his rope. And Joan of Arc was permitted to keep her stake, as long as she remained firmly tied to it.

Security agents surrounded the new grand duke as he mingled with his guests in the festively decorated gardens. The orchestra was in top form and the ball proceeded without a hitch—until fire broke out in the royal archives.

150

The archives, a small stone building in a secluded corner of the palace grounds, held the tiny nation's most revered, and highly flammable, documents. The fire was soon put out, but the documents had all been irretrievably ruined—a strong psychological victory for the rebels.

Hercules (chief of the secret police) borrowed a magnifying glass from Sherlock Holmes (royal stable master) and examined the damaged archive building. A stream of sunlight poured through the archive's only window, still intact and locked from the inside. And the only key to the only door was safe in the duke's jacket pocket. "The fire started from inside," Hercules moaned. "That much is clear. And yet no one could have gotten inside."

Napoleon (the prime minister) gazed about at the assembled guests. "I can guess how it was done," announced the clever politician. "And only one person could have done it."

Whodunit? And how?

Solution on page 332

A Winter's Tale

In the dead of winter, the citizens of Mountebank, Minnesota, grabbed at any excuse for a party, especially when it was hosted by Ama Wheeler, the richest woman in town. As usual, this one was rowdy and crowded and a huge success—until about 12:30 A.M. That's when Ama noticed that her prized Ming vase was missing from the entry-hall table.

When the police arrived, they found all the revelers herded into the living room, with Ama standing guard like an angry sheepdog. The house was searched. Then the house perimeter. Then the guests' cars. No vase.

"You're going to have to take their statements," Ama told the police chief. "I don't suppose it will do much good. At a party like this, people can barely remember their own movements, much less keep track of others'."

Philip McGlass stepped forward with his state-

153

ment. "I was one of the first to arrive, about the same time as Julie Becker. I never once left the house. If people don't remember me it's because I spent half the party in a bedroom, watching a basketball game." The chief took down Philip's information, then told him he could go.

Rod Shallowitz was next. "I have to get home," he apologized. "If I'm not there for the twins' two o'clock feeding, my wife will have my head." Rod also claimed never to have left the premises. "Oh," he recalled. "No. I did step out onto a second-story balcony, but it was so bitter cold I came right back in."

Julie Becker was the third to make a statement. She also claimed to have never left and seen nothing. "I spent much of the party flitting from group to group and munching at the various food tables." The chief dismissed her, too, and watched as she went into the hall and grabbed her coat from the top of a crowded coat rack.

"This is going to take all night," Ama complained.

The chief disagreed. "No. I think I have a viable suspect already."

Strangulation Station

Colonel Rollo's tour of the provinces was a necessary evil and the military dictator took every precaution to ensure his own safety. There had already been two assassination attempts this year, and he didn't want to try for three.

When the colonel's train pulled into the Gorganzuela station, the town officials were waiting to greet him. But the door to his windowless, bullet-proof carriage remained shut. Nervously, the mayor knocked. He heard some stumbling sounds from inside and finally the train door slid open.

Captain Corkran stumbled out. The dictator's second in command was usually a resplendent sight in his broad hat, bandanna, and American cowboy boots. Now he looked weak and silly. "Assassination," he coughed.

The mayor looked in and saw the lifeless body of Colonel Rollo dressed in his robe and slippers.

A purple ring around his lifeless neck testified to murder by strangulation, probably with a long, strong, thin cord.

The dictator's bodyguard lay unconscious on the floor. He was revived and told his story. "We were all in different parts of the car. I was at my post by the door. Captain Corkran was at his desk, Colonel Rollo was napping, and Madam Rollo was in the bathroom putting on makeup." The bodyguard kicked the wall in frustration and his combat boots made a dent. "I don't know how it happened. All of a sudden, the car was filled with smoke. In mere seconds, we were all unconscious."

The train's engineer had seen nothing unusual and the three surviving passengers all told the same story. Each had been alone when the smoke bomb exploded.

A thorough search produced only one clue: a gas mask. There was no murder weapon and no clue to how the assassin got in and out. "A phantom," moaned the elegantly dressed widow with a shudder. "Like retribution from heaven."

"No," said the clever mayor. "It was a very real

assassin, someone who must have brought the murder weapon on board. In fact, I think I see it now."

Who killed the dictator and what was the weapon?

Solution on page 338

The Suicidal Schemer

"Avery Archer was involved in some shady deals," the homicide sergeant said as he gazed down at the body. "Maybe that's why he committed suicide."

It certainly looked like suicide. The businessman in question was slumped back in his office chair, his hands folded peacefully in his lap. The murder weapon, a revolver, had fallen onto the desk, right beside a box of cough drops. The victim had been shot in the back of the mouth at the closest range possible. "It's near impossible to shoot someone in the throat," the sergeant continued. "Especially when there's absolutely no sign of a struggle."

The man's secretary provided background. "Avery was depressed, partly on account of his lingering cold. Also, a few of his investors were getting suspicious. One even threatened to call the police fraud squad. Avery was working frantically

161

to salvage this one deal. He had a noon appointment today with an investor; I don't know which. When I went to lunch, the investor still hadn't arrived. When I came back, Avery was just like that. Gruesome."

The police checked the contracts and discovered that this particular deal had three investors: Gino Grimaldi, a suspected mob figure; Marie Lackaday, the owner of a chain of gun stores; and Dr. Pete Crocus, a general internist.

"One of these three kept the noon appointment with our victim," the sergeant hypothesized. "The investor threatened him with exposure and ruin—so Avery Archer killed himself."

"Not quite." The homicide captain had held his tongue until now. "This was definitely murder, not suicide. And I have a good hunch who did it."

Why does he suspect murder? And who is the most likely suspect?

Solution on page 339

A Theatrical Threat

Sir Mortimer Gains leaned across and confided a secret. "This is an exclusive, just for the *Times*. After talking with my new wife and with Alex Toinby, my costar, I have decided to leave the London production of *Willy Boy* and accept a movie offer in Hollywood. As you know, my bride is American. She's never really gotten used to England."

The reporter was aghast. "But what about your fans here? What about the play? Can it keep running without you?"

Sir Mortimer shrugged. "My producer has agreed to let me out of my contract. Now, if you'll excuse me . . ." He motioned toward the dressing room door. "It takes an hour of makeup and preparation before each show." Thrilled to have such a scoop, the reporter rushed out of the King Edward Theatre to file his story.

Sir Mortimer went on that evening to give his

164

usual, brilliant performance. After acknowledging ten curtain calls, he returned to his dressing room. A handwritten note was on his makeup table.

"I won't let you take your talents elsewhere. I'd rather see you dead than have you dishonor the British theater. It may take the form of a bomb in your car trunk or poison in your favorite whiskey. But make no mistake; if you go to Hollywood, I will kill you.—A Fan."

The morning *Times* now had two sensational stories to report: the defection of Sir Mortimer and the threat by a deranged fan.

William Cathgate, the play's producer, was worried. "You should reconsider," he told the actor. "If you want to do film work, do it here. I'll give you the weeks free. Just do four performances every weekend."

Alex Toinby agreed. "The Americans won't appreciate your talent. You'll wind up running around in stupid action films."

Sir Mortimer didn't know what to do. And then a voice spoke from the dressing room shadows. "I don't think Sir Mortimer has much to worry about," said the Scotland Yard detective. "I pretty much know who sent him that note."

Whom does the detective suspect?

Solution on page 341

A Hard Day's Night

Clive pulled into his driveway, tired and cranky. When he'd taken this job with Gotham Advertising, he knew he'd be working long and hard, but he never expected to be arriving home at 8:30 A.M. With any luck, he could still get in a few hours' sleep before this afternoon's presentation. Clive climbed the porch. He had just put the key in the lock when he heard a noise behind him.

The police arrived ten minutes later, alerted by neighbors who'd heard a gunshot. They found a young businessman dressed in a torn and bloody suit and with a briefcase on the porch by his side. They also found a key chain suspended from the front-door lock and a bullet hole in the young man's chest.

"Looks like a botched robbery," the rookie officer told his partner. "Poor guy must have put up a struggle." He stooped to pick up a nearly empty wallet. "Clive Custard," he read from the driver's

license.

The officers began by looking for witnesses. A taxi had been seen in the area. They tracked down the driver, told him all the facts they knew, then asked for his help. "I'd just dropped off a passenger," the cabby told them. "Maybe two blocks away. I had the window down and I heard something—like a car backfiring. It was a minute or two after 8:30. I didn't see anything—except this parcel delivery truck."

The police found the delivery man and gave him the same briefing. "Poor guy," he said shaking his head. "Someone must've followed him home. Unfortunately, I didn't see or hear a thing. I keep the radio playing in my truck, and when I'm in there sorting boxes I can't hear much."

The officers compared notes. "We're going to have to check with Custard's friends and associates," the rookie concluded. "If they tell us what I think, then we already have our killer."

Whom do they suspect? And why?

Solution on page 319

Myra's Three Sons

Inspector Matthews glanced around the kitchen of the weekend cottage. There was cold coffee in the coffemaker, an ice cube tray half filled with melting cubes, and just a trace of ash in an ashtray. "All right, Mrs. Thurl. Tell me again."

The next-door neighbor looked uncomfortable. "I had just come home. It was about 8 P.M. I heard a car pull into the driveway next door. I mean here, at this house. When I looked out, two people had arrived and were walking toward the kitchen door. I recognized the woman. Myra Lovesy is rather fat—was. The man I couldn't see. They were fighting. The man grabbed Myra by the throat. She collapsed in a heap. Then the man just unlocked the door and walked inside. It took you long enough to get here—fifteen minutes from the time I called."

Myra Lovesy's three grown sons were in the house when the police arrived. "The place had

been closed up for the past month," Sherman Lovesy testified. "I arrived early this afternoon. No one else was here. I parked in the garage. Then I went down to the basement to turn on the electricity. In the kitchen, I smoked a cigarette. Then I went up to my room and took a nap. You guys woke me up."

"I was the first to arrive," his brother Donald protested. "I parked behind the cottage. The electricity had never been turned off. We often neglected to do it. I made coffee, then took a cup into the library. I guess I fell asleep."

The third brother also declared his early arrival. "I parked in the garage," Luther said. "Sherman's car was not in the other bay. I went into the basement, turned on the electricity, then came up and made myself a cocktail. Mother said she would be arriving with one of the other boys."

The inspector reviewed his notes. One of them was lying. One of the sons had driven his mother to the cottage, fought with her by the kitchen door, and strangled her to death.

Whodunit?

Solution on page 327

A Nun Too Pretty Murder

Harriet Murmer was scheduled to testify against her ex-husband, a capo in the Domino crime family. The FBI had to keep their witness safe and they chose the Convent of Perpetual Solitude, a walled, all-women enclave in the heart of Manhattan. It was perfect. No self-respecting mobster would dare shoot up a community of nuns.

On the second week of Harriet's stay, the FBI's confidence was shattered—as was their case, as was Harriet's skull—by a shell from a .44 magnum. Just as the sisters were gathering for evening vespers, a gunshot echoed through the convent's stone archways. Sister Margaret Mary announced the news. Her tight, starched collar bobbed up and down as she gulped. "Ms. Murmer is dead."

The FBI found their witness in her room on the third floor. "I don't know how an assassin could have gotten in and out without anyone seeing him." Mother Superior shivered.

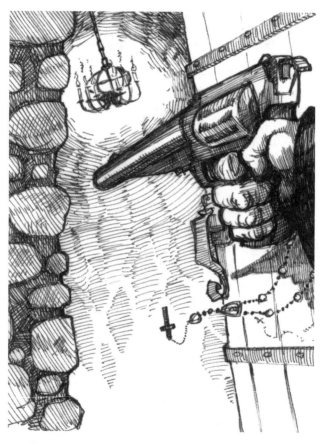

"Maybe he didn't get in and out," special agent McCormack replied. "Have any new sisters arrived recently?"

In fact, there were three new arrivals. Sister Margaret Mary was from Cleveland. "I was on the second floor when I heard the shot," the older nun said. "I hid in a corner, in the shadows, more frightened for myself than for our poor guest. A few seconds later, I saw Sister Juliana coming down from the third floor. She didn't see me, but I definitely saw a gun in her hand. After she passed by, I went upstairs and found the body."

Sister Juliana was a transfer from Patterson, New Jersey, and admitted to carrying a .22 handgun. "When my brother heard I was coming here, he made me take it. Seems he was right. When I heard the shot, I grabbed my gun and headed downstairs. I didn't see a thing."

Sister Ursula had been in a third-floor bathroom. After the shot, she claimed to have heard a man's voice, talking to himself as he walked down the hall. She was the last to arrive at the vespers chapel.

Whom should the FBI hold for further questioning?

Solution on page 328

Three Weak Alibis

After two straight days of dark skies, the stationary front moved, bathing the city of Seattle in bright sunshine. The change seemed to put everyone in a good mood. Well, almost everyone. Fifteen minutes after the sun broke through, a gunshot rang out in the offices of Claxton & Brightman, attorneys-at-law.

As luck would have it, a trio of security guards just happened to be sitting in the Claxton & Brightman reception area. The guards barreled through an inner door and down the hall. The firm's senior partner, Henry Claxton, lay in a pool of blood in his office, most decidedly dead.

Without exchanging a word, the experienced guards broke up, looking for anyone who might have seen anything. Only three offices were occupied and each occupant had a story.

"I heard Claxton arguing with someone," Annette Goulding told guard number one. "I was

reviewing court documents and I tried to mentally block out the sound."

The guard saw the red light blinking on Annette's voice-mail system and asked how long she'd been here in her office. "For nearly an hour," she replied. "When I'm busy I don't answer my phone."

Meanwhile, the second guard was talking to George Brightman, the firm's surviving partner. "As you can see, Henry's office is way on the other side. I heard nothing until the gunshot. Then I opened my door and looked out into the hall. I heard running footsteps but didn't see anyone." The guard noticed that George's window was open, allowing a warm breeze to play through the blinds.

The third guard was with the firm's youngest lawyer, Ellen Youst. "I've been holed up here for hours, working on a speech I'm delivering tonight." She pointed to her computer, the screen awash in sunlight from the window. Ellen swiveled it so the guard could see. It certainly looked like a boring, lawyerly speech.

While the receptionist called the police, the guards compared notes. "All their alibis seem weak," said guard number two. "But one of them is definitely lying."

Whom does he suspect and why?

Solution on page 343

Bye-Bye, Bully

A lot of towns have their neighborhood bullies. But few neighborhood bullies were as hated as Pete Weider of Cozy Heights and, luckily for the crime statistics, even fewer wound up like Peter.

A passing patrol car heard the screams and responded immediately. They found the burly corpse in his own backyard, with multiple stab wounds. There were signs of a struggle, and blood was everywhere around the fenced-in yard. The officers immediately went to question the neighbors and were surprised to discover that not a single one had heard or seen a thing.

"They're lying, of course," the homicide captain said when he heard the news. At least three men on the block had been outside when the murder occurred and the captain insisted on talking to them as soon as possible.

Blake Fromm had just finished painting his porch when the captain approached. A young,

182

genial man, Blake wiped his hands on his nearly spotless jeans before shaking hands. The captain immediately noticed the cassette player on Blake's belt and the earphones draped around his neck. "I've been outside all morning. The porch ceiling took forever. Pete lives two doors away. I really didn't hear or see anything," he added apologetically.

Nelson Olson had been in his garden, right next door to the victim's yard. "I was in and out of the house. Weeding. Planting bulbs for the fall." There was dirt on his hands and under his nails. "Inside, I had the air conditioner cranked up. It all must have happened when I was indoors. Sorry."

Kenny Kitchner's story was even less plausible. "I was on a ladder, washing my windows," the paunchy, middle-aged man admitted. His T-shirt was still wet. The captain could see that Kenny's yard overlooked the victim's. "I never looked over into Pete Weider's yard, nor did I hear anything. I had other things on my mind."

"Two of those guys are just lying," the captain muttered. "Protecting the killer. And I think I

Maria's Last Clue

Sergeant Vacca had been on the homicide squad for eight years and had never once run into a deathbed clue. Not once had he heard a dying man blurt out the name of his killer or seen him grab at his St. Christopher medal in order to incriminate a suspect named Chris. Even though he was a devout mystery fan, Sergeant Vacca had begun to seriously doubt that such things ever really happened. Until now.

His captain was still skeptical. "Who says this is a deathbed clue? Looks like a bunch of gibberish." The gibberish consisted of two words typed on a computer screen.

The police had found Maria Consuela alone in her downtown office cubicle. The attractive legal secretary had stayed late to finish typing up a brief and had been rewarded with a blunt object to the head and ribs. There was no sign of forced entry and little sign of struggle—an indication that she

186

had known her attacker.

A pool of blood trailed away from the cubicle's doorway and ended in Maria's collapsed body, right under the edge of her desk. "It must have taken her last ounce of strength to crawl over here," Sergeant Vacca theorized. "She must have had some reason."

He gazed again at the computer screen. The last thing typed was a line of legal jargon transcribed from her boss's legal pad. The line ended abruptly in mid-sentence and was followed by two nonsensical words: "48dy 28oo8qjw."

"Forget the gibberish," ordered the captain. "Let's concentrate on her male co-workers. Office gossip says Maria was having an affair with one of them." He checked his notepad. "We have Richard Williams, Gary Hallardi, and Paul Cattalgo. Check on 'em."

"Wait a minute," Vacca said as he stared at the names. "I know who it was. Good old Maria did leave us a message."

Whom does Vacca suspect and what does the message mean?

Solution on page 326

The Telltale Prints

The homicide officers tromped through the morning mud to the main tent of the Big Top Circus. The ringmaster was waiting. He led them around to the rear and pointed to the stacked bags of elephant chow just outside the tent flaps. When the officers peered over the top, they saw Aeriel Cummings lying facedown in the mud.

Aeriel was in her circus costume, loosely covered in a robe. Even from this distance, the officers could see the welts around her neck. The hand marks were clear on her pale skin, the outline of two thumbs pointing down toward her bare shoulders.

"Strangled," the ringmaster explained needlessly. "It poured heavy last night, starting around 2 A.M. This morning I checked for rain damage. That's when I found her. Aeriel is our star acrobat. She does a balancing act with her partner, Rudolph."

189

Before approaching the body, the officers checked the wet ground and saw prints of the ringmaster's pointy boots all around the body. The only other footprints were a huge set, at least a size 20, just outside the bags of elephant chow. "We'll need to talk to your clowns."

It didn't take long to track the prints to Smiley Cummings, the head clown and Aeriel's sour, dry-eyed husband. "I kept telling her, 'You play with men the way you do and you're asking for trouble.' I guess someone finally took her flirting seriously."

Aeriel's partner confirmed her reputation. "As far as I know, it was all just flirting," Rudolph said kindly. "Aeriel was with me last night after the show, practicing a new trick. We finished up around midnight. Then I guess she went back to Smiley's trailer."

But Smiley said she never arrived. "When she didn't come home, I put on the nearest pair of shoes, clown shoes, and I went out looking. I circled the tent, but I didn't see her. Of course, I wasn't looking for her on the ground hidden behind some bags."

The senior officer returned to the rear flap, studying the corpse and the two sets of footprints. "It seems pretty clear who did it."

Whodunit and how did he know?

Solution on page 341

The Kidnapping Killer

"Hi, Mom." It was Alice Grunwald's voice. "I guess you're in the shower. I . . . Wait a minute. Someone's at the door. Anyway, I'll see you at six." The answering machine clicked off, then gave the time of the message, 3:32 P.M.

At six, Mrs. Grunwald arrived at her daughter's apartment. She was looking forward to dinner and hearing about Alice's boyfriend troubles. When Alice didn't answer, she used her own key. There was no one at home. Mrs. Grunwald's heart stopped as she saw blood on the entry hall carpet and a note on the table—a ransom note.

Mrs. Grunwald immediately called the police, who discovered a large amount of blood in one of the building's elevators. More was found in the basement, leading them to check behind the boilers. That's where they found Alice's body. She had been stabbed once and died almost instantly. The coroner set the time of death between 3:30 and

193

4:00, shortly after the unknown visitor had knocked on Alice's door.

Fernando, the building's janitor, was interviewed. "No one came down to the basement while I was on duty. I get off at 5:30. That's no secret. There's a big notice in the lobby saying so."

The police soon had a theory: The killer couldn't leave Alice's body in the apartment, not if he wanted ransom money. And he couldn't remove her through the lobby. He had to wait up in her apartment, with the dead body, until Fernando was off duty. Then he went down and hid her in the basement.

Alice, a rich girl, had always been attracted to shady boyfriends, and suspicion soon fell on her two most recent. Both had partial alibis.

Her current beau, Chip, had been out shopping. A credit card receipt showed that at 4:16 he had been miles away, charging a cart full of items at a hardware store.

Her ex-boyfriend, Dale, had an alibi from 4:45 onward, when he showed up for an appointment at a nearby hair salon.

The chief investigator reviewed all the statements, then took one person downtown for further questioning.

Whom? And why?

Solution on page 321

The Gypsy Thief

Dahlia shuffled the deck, making the bracelet of coins tinkle on her right wrist. Dealing out the first card, she smiled. "You had good luck," she said, pointing to the Queen of Cups.

Marco patted his leather purse. It looked heavy with coins. "I had a good morning at the fair. No one sells like a Gypsy."

It was a tranquil afternoon as they sat around the embers of a fire in their small encampment. The sound of horse hooves and jangling spurs announced the arrival of Renard. Seconds later, Carmen's earrings, as melodious as wind chimes and almost as large, told them that their fourth friend had also returned.

The tiny Gypsy tribe exchanged tales of their morning escapades. Dahlia had told fortunes at the fair. Carmen had begged on a street corner. Renard had traded horses with local farmers. But the only lucky one was Marco, who had sold cop-

per pots to housewives and made an enviable profit.

The warm air was still, with not even a bird song to break the quiet. Perfect for an afternoon doze. The Gypsies retreated to separate corners of the encampment, nestled back against a tree and settled into leisurely naps.

Three of the Gypsy friends were awakened by a yelp from the fourth. Marco was standing in the middle of the clearing, cursing as he held up the cut ends of his purse strings. "What is the world coming to when you can't even trust a fellow Gypsy? One of you low dogs stole my money."

Dahlia reached out her left hand. Her bracelet jangled annoyingly as she examined the strings. The cuts were clean. "Cut by a horse-shoeing knife," she said and glanced up at Renard.

The horse dealer bristled. "No. It could have been a paring knife. Carmen was peeling an apple just before she went to sleep. And what about Dahlia's scissors?"

"Ha!" Carmen snarled. "No one could be so stealthy as to rob a Gypsy. If you ask me, it was Marco himself."

Chili con Carnage

The murder should have been discovered at 7 A.M. That's when Gil Caster's assistant, Marie, was supposed to arrive at his Austin, Texas, home and start helping him prepare for the biggest night of his career, the Governor's Chili con Carne Ball.

But Marie and Gil had had a fight just the night before and Marie had quit, leaving Gil's estranged wife, a local television reporter, to find the body at 3 P.M. when she and her crew showed up to interview him. Before the police even arrived, a tearful Aretha Caster was live on the air, reporting the death of her own husband: "Just minutes ago, Texas's most famous down-home chef was found in his kitchen, apparently hacked to death with a meat cleaver. In what can only be described as a cruel afterthought, the unknown killer stuffed the murdered man, head first, into his own chili pot."

That night at eight, the Governor's dinner went on as scheduled, thanks in large part to Austin's

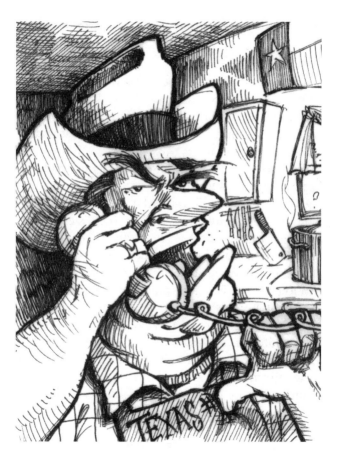

201

second-best chili chef, an opportunist named Winston Short. "As soon as I heard the news, I threw the pinto beans in to soak, mixed up the corn bread mash, and telephoned the Governor's Office, offering my services. I would've liked to give the spices more time to simmer, but I think we all understand the unfortunate circumstances I was working under."

Even as the ballroom full of VIP's were gorging themselves on Winston's savory beans and meat, the Austin police were busy interviewing Marie. "Gil was using my family recipe for his chili," the ex-assistant told them. "He promised to give me credit in the ball's menu. But last night I found out he hadn't done any such thing. I called him up and quit, right over the phone. I haven't been to his house since the day before yesterday."

The police reviewed the evidence and brought in a suspect for question.

Whom? And what made them suspicious?

Solution on page 307

The Playboy's Empty Vase

Morton was a bad influence. So was Archie. And that's probably why they were such good friends. The two playboys had simultaneously squandered their trust funds and now were facing the consequences.

"I suppose I'll have to start selling things," Morton said with a shiver. He had just arrived home from a night on the town. "Want to come in for a drink, old man?"

Never one to say no, Archie followed his friend inside. Morton's trusted valet, Gene, was there to pour their drinks and watch as his employer removed his diamond cufflinks and tossed them into an empty vase in the library.

Archie stayed for one drink, complained about his own financial straits, then headed out into the damp night air. Morton exited the house a minute later, taking his German shepherd for a walk that they both felt they could use.

It was only a short while later when a police squad car passed by on a routine patrol and spotted a suspicious-looking character on the terrace. It was Archie.

"My car wouldn't start," Archie told the officers. "I was just about to walk back here to call the garage when I heard glass breaking." He pointed to the shards of broken glass on the terrace and then to the hole in the terrace's French doors. The glass pane right above the latch had been smashed and the door stood open. "Looks like a burglar."

When Morton came in from walking the dog, he found one police officer searching his friend and the other searching the library. He also found the diamond cufflinks missing from the library vase.

"We caught him almost red-handed," the senior officer told Morton. "But we can't find the cufflinks. Were they insured?"

"Yes, of course," Morton replied. "Just look at the mess you've made." He pointed to the muddy footprints they'd tracked in from the garden. "If there was any evidence of a real burglar, you've completely obliterated it."

But Morton was wrong. There was one piece of evidence. And it pointed straight to the thief.

Whodunit? And what was the evidence?

Solution on page 331

The Emery Emerald

Mrs. Emery was disappointed. She had assumed that dealers at a gem exposition would know how to dress. But the room was filled with fashion mistakes. Rodney Dipp from Boston had on a polyester shirt; not the good, new kind of polyester, but something left over from the seventies. Julia Kidd from Atlanta wore sneakers and something resembling an upscale jogging suit. Even Klaus Braun from Düsseldorf, usually known for his style, was wearing one brown sock and one blue sock.

"Well, at least I'm maintaining my standards," Mrs. Emery huffed as she laid out her unmounted gems. The display was not as impressive as it had been in years past. The only great gem she had left for sale was an exquisite emerald. She did her best, nestling the brilliant stone in an arrangement of loose gems—aquamarines, sapphires of poor color, lowly garnets, and a few bloodstones—hop-

208

ing that the emerald's luster might somehow reflect into the lesser stones.

The theft took place during a diversion. A minor but noisy traffic accident drew the crowd out onto the street. When the insatiably curious Mrs. Emery returned to her display table, she found it all gone—everything from the almost worthless garnets up to the most prized gem at the show, her beloved emerald.

"The thief obviously had an accomplice," the police captain told the robbed gem dealer. "Someone who staged the diversion. Unfortunately, we don't know who that was. But we do have this."

The captain opened a cloth pouch and Mrs. Emery gasped. There were her gems, dozens of bright, glittering stones. All of them were there, except the emerald.

"We found these in an alley two blocks away," the captain reported. "Looks like the emerald was the only one they wanted."

Mrs. Emery looked at the gems, then smiled. "It had to be another dealer. We were the only ones in the room. And I'm pretty sure I know who it was."

Whom does she suspect? And why?

Solution on page 313

The Bad Samaritan

Stan Rogers winced at the flesh wound in his left shoulder, feeling lucky to be alive. "My partner and I were delivering a payroll to the logging camp," he told the officers at his hospital bedside. "It was late at night when the car broke down. I pulled over. Benny got out but I stayed inside. Those are the rules.

"A minute later, a passing motorist stopped to help. Benny and this guy checked the engine, fiddling with the connections. A couple times it almost started. I couldn't see their faces because they were standing right in front and the headlights were slung low. But I saw when the guy pulled the gun from his jacket.

"He shot Benny in the chest, just like that. Benny stumbled off to the side and collapsed. The guy came around to the driver's side. Me, I kept trying to start the engine. He must have known about the payroll 'cause he opened the rear door

and grabbed it right off the backseat. He slammed the door and was coming up to me when the engine finally turned over. I slipped it in gear just as he got a shot off." Stan winced again. "Gee, if I hadn't run into you guys I might've fainted or bled to death."

The highway patrol brought in two lone motorists whose cars fit the description Stan had given of the killer's vehicle. Neither suspect had the payroll bag, and the murder weapon was found back at the scene, wiped clean of prints. The only hope for an arrest lay in Stan's memory.

The first suspect was tall, with a blond crew cut and a small spider web tattoo on his right wrist. The second suspect was shorter and left-handed. His hair was also short, but dark. Stan examined photographs of both clean-shaven men, but could not make an identification.

The senior officer led the way out of Stan's hospital room. "From what he told us about the attacker, I think it's clear who it was."

Whodunit? And what gave him away?

Solution on page 305

Tornado Allie

The air in Prairie Flats had been calm all morning. But by noon the wind had whipped up out of the east, and just a half-hour later a small, rainless tornado was pummeling the farming community, its funnel leaving behind a path of destruction and at least one fatality.

The body of Allie Brinker was found lying in a ditch. There was a gash in the young woman's forehead and a trickle of blood that had fallen in neat round drops onto the ground. Not far away, a broken, bloodied fence post led the police to an obvious conclusion. The wind had torn up the post and sent it flying into her head.

"I blame myself," Allie's Uncle Nate told the neighbors. "She was at my place, playing with her one-year-old niece. Just as the wind was picking up, Allie decided to run back home across the fields. I told her to stay. The radio was warning of twisters. I should have stopped her."

After the tornado passed, Allie's boyfriend, Josh, had gone out looking for her. "Last night we had a fight," Josh moaned. "I wanted to make up. But no one knew where Allie was. I had a feeling something bad must have happened. I must have driven past the field twice, but I never saw her in that ditch."

It was Allie's older sister, Beth, who discovered the body. "I was on my way to Uncle Nate's to pick up my daughter. The wind was still strong, so I took the path down by the long ditch where it's easier to walk. I almost fell over her." Beth was still shivering from the horrible shock.

The authorities were all prepared to call it accidental, a tragic example of nature's fury. But then a young deputy sheriff noticed something, a clue that not only told them it was murder but who the most likely suspect would be.

Whodunit? And what was the clue?

Solution on page 344

A Housewarming Theft

Miranda Rich could hardly wait to move into her new house. In fact, a trio of workmen were still making their final repairs and installations on that April morning when Miranda brought over her expensive entertainment system and stacked it in a corner of the living room.

The next day, Miranda arrived to find the electronic unit gone. The only thing left behind was a strip of black plastic tape the burglar had used to hold open the latch of the rear kitchen door.

"Looks like a crime of opportunity," the officer from the burglary unit told her. "All three workmen were here and saw the system. All three of them heard you on the telephone, setting up a dinner date for last night. Knowing the house would be empty, one of them simply taped open the latch and came back later."

No fingerprints had been left behind, and the officer didn't hold out much hope. But he inter-

viewed the suspects anyway, hoping two of them would have ironclad alibis.

"I was at Philharmonic Hall," Pete the plumber testified, and showed off a torn ticket stub. "None of my friends like the symphony so I always go alone. They were doing Beethoven's Ninth with a full chorus—a not-to-be-missed experience."

Ed the electrician had gone to the movies. He didn't have a stub, but the movie had just opened last night and he could repeat the entire plot and half of the jokes. "After the movie I went straight home. I'm an early riser and I need my sleep."

Max the painter had rented a video and bought take-out Chinese food. "I was going to spend a quiet evening with my girlfriend at home. But she canceled on me. "You know," Max added. "I was working in Ms. Rich's kitchen most of yesterday, and I didn't see anything suspicious. Of course, I left before the other guys did."

The officer reviewed the evidence, then called in one of the workers for further questioning.

Whom does he suspect? And why?

Solution on page 320

Which Dewdit Did It?

The lawyer glanced from his client to the three greedy young faces across the room. "You're sure you want to do this?"

"Of course," Derwood Dewdit replied. "I have no children. It's only right that my niece and nephews inherit my estate."

"That won't be for many, many years," Asa Dewdit said. His sister Bebe agreed as did brother Cecil. They watched, fascinated, as Uncle Derwood signed his new will.

Nothing happened until late afternoon. The lawyer was browsing through the books in the third-floor library when he heard Derwood's voice raised in a blood-curdling scream. For a few seconds, he sat in shock. Then he bounded down the stairs.

He found Asa on the second floor, standing at the top of the little-used back staircase. "It came from the first floor," stammered the young heir.

The lawyer took the lead down the narrow stairs. "Derwood!" he shouted and a moment later caught a spider web across his face.

The kitchen was right at the bottom. The white marble floor was spotless and still damp from a recent mopping by the maid. The adjacent pantry, however, was quite messy. Derwood Dewdit lay on the pantry floor. He'd been stabbed to death with a paring knife.

The lawyer was careful not to disturb anything. Using a handkerchief, he tried the kitchen door. Unlocked. Looking out into the garden, he could see a path of footprints in the mud, leading right up to the kitchen door and then away again. "Call the police."

The Dewdits and the lawyer all retired to the parlor to await the authorities. "An intruder must have come in the back way," Cecil said emphatically. "I was sitting in the front hall by the main stairs. I didn't see anyone."

"Me neither," Bebe said, absently fingering the mud on her shoes. "I was strolling around the garden, right by the kitchen. I didn't see a thing. Do you think it might be one of us?"

"Of course it was," the lawyer snarled. "And I can guess which one."

Whodunit?

Solution on page 348

The Pretenders' Ball, III

Two years ago, the Pretenders' Ball had been the scene of an assassination. Last year, an arsonist destroyed the royal archives. These political crimes, carried out by the rebel forces, were becoming a regular part of the Grand Duchy's annual costume ball. The chief of police pleaded with the prime minister to cancel this year's event. Naturally, he didn't. For added security, though, he did change the location to Duchy Park, a floral wonderland surrounded by a high, unscalable stone wall.

Upon entry, Robin Hood's arrows were confiscated, although he was allowed to keep his bow and quiver. David had to give up his slingshot and Goliath handed over his club. Mary Poppins kept her umbrella, but Death turned in his scythe. Even the clown was searched. One guard held onto his big bunch of balloons while another checked inside his oversized shoes.

225

The festive nighttime ball went on as scheduled. The music played, the costumed revelers danced, and champagne corks popped. Something else popped, too—a small derringer pistol.

The victim this time was the Grand Duchy's chief of police, dressed as a Chicago gangster, the only guest actually allowed to carry a weapon. His body was found in the middle of a hedge maze, the gun in his shoulder holster untouched.

"Shot in the back," Death (the royal physician) reported. "Very small caliber. Anyone could have sneaked in a gun that size."

In what was becoming another annual tradition, the guests lined up to be frisked. The prime minister observed them: Mary Poppins leaning on her umbrella; Goliath looking chilly in his leopard skin; the clown looking sullen, both hands stuffed in his pockets. Two hours later, the results came in. There was no gun, not anywhere in the park. The guards around the park's perimeter reported that nothing had been thrown over the wall.

"I know how our assassin could have gotten rid of the gun," the prime minister deduced. "And that tells me who our assassin probably is."

Whodunit? And how did the gun disappear?

Solution on page 333

The Nutty Strangler

The newspapers dubbed him that, the nutty strangler, although there was nothing funny about him. Five times he'd struck, each time leaving nut shells—piles of nut shells. On the first occasion the body of a businessman was found in an alley. The police barely noticed the walnut shells among the midtown litter.

The second time it was a suburban housewife and peanut shells. On the third strangulation (a secretary and pecans) the homicide squad started looking at photos of the previous cases. That's when they made the connection.

"Maybe he likes nuts," a rookie suggested. "Maybe cracking shells calms this psycho down while he waits for the right victim to come by."

On the sixth murder, the police caught a break. It was late. Four officers were just coming off their shift when they heard a strangled scream. They arrived too late to save the young college

229

student. But one glance at the piles of red pistachio shells told them who they were dealing with. The officers fanned out, detaining the only three men they could find in the surrounding streets.

The first was a homeless man, discovered sleeping over a steam vent. There was no alcohol on his breath. The man claimed to have been living on the street for only a week. The police examined his hands. They were large and clean and strong-looking.

The second was a man in a suit, claiming to be on his way home from the office. "I know the subway's in the other direction," he admitted. "But when I heard the scream I got scared. The street here is better lighted."

The third was working on his car. "It broke down a few minutes ago," he said, pulling his grease-covered hands out from under the hood. "You can try to start her if you don't believe me. I was all set to call AAA."

A sergeant turned to his companions. "I think I know who it is. But there's an easy way to find out for sure."

Whom does he suspect? How can he prove it?

Solution on page 328

230

Hand in the Cookie Jar

Valerie stretched her six-foot frame to the top shelf, looking for a hiding place. Taking down an old cookie jar, she slipped in the roll of hundred-dollar bills, then lifted it back up to its spot above the kitchen cabinets. Valerie flipped aside a lock of golden hair. It was a shame to have to hide things in her own house, but with this bunch of sorry losers visiting for the weekend, it was better safe than—well—sorry.

It was a horrible thing to think about her best friend. Sometimes she didn't know what she saw in Glenda. Glenda was strikingly homely, dumpy, and of dubious moral character. But she seemed to admire Valerie and made her laugh.

It was even worse to think about her own twin brother, but Valerie had to be honest. Ever since childhood, Victor had regularly stolen from any purse that happened to be lying around.

The third guest, Morton Flyer, had been a bas-

ketball star in the NBA. Caught red-handed in a betting scandal, Morton had been thrown out of the sport. He and Victor were now best buddies, sharing their mutual hobbies of gambling and drinking.

Just as Valerie finished putting the jar back in place, a slight noise caught her attention. She spun around, but no one was there. All the same, she felt uneasy.

In the middle of a restless night's sleep, Valerie thought she heard a noise. Going downstairs to check it out, she stubbed her toe on a chair, out of place by the kitchen counter. Immediately, Valerie feared the worst, switched on the light, then checked the cookie jar. The money, all of it, was gone.

She examined the kitchen. An empty beer bottle was in the sink, and on the counter lay a short strand of blond hair, not unlike her own. She remembered emptying the garbage right before bedtime. But in the trash bin now were another beer bottle and two bottle caps.

Valerie scanned the kitchen again and suddenly she knew.

Around-the-Clock Murder

It was 8:50 P.M. and Jules Marigold was closing up shop. The antique dealer wound all the clocks while his employees tallied up the receipts. When Marigold tried setting the alarm, he was annoyed to find it out of order. "Oh, well," he sighed. "I suppose one night without an alarm won't kill me." He was wrong.

Around midnight, when the Downtown Citizens' Patrol shone their flashlights through the storefront window, they saw a chaotic mess. Lying in the middle of the mess was the bludgeoned body of Jules Marigold.

Marigold lived above his shop. The police theorized that he'd heard a burglar breaking in and that the two men had fought. Among the wreckage was a toppled, broken grandfather clock. The hands had stopped at 11:09. "I guess that sets the time of the murder."

Since there was no sign of forced entry, the

236

police concentrated on the only people with keys, Marigold's employees.

George Lafleur had been the first to leave. "I had a 9 P.M. class," he explained. "Antique appraising. I'm planning to open my own business." The professor remembered George. He also remembered ending the class at 10:45, giving George enough time to make it back to the shop and commit murder.

Charlie Weed said he'd walked home, changed clothes, then gone out to a nearby dance club. The club doorman recalled Charlie perfectly. "At 11 we start charging a cover. This guy seemed real proud for getting here a minute early and saving himself five bucks." The bartenders also recalled Charlie, who nursed the same drink for over an hour.

Derrick Posie had left the shop to have dinner alone at his favorite cafe. The owner knew Derrick well and estimated that the young, lonely clerk finished his meal shortly after 10:30.

The forensics squad dusted the scene. Prints of Marigold and his employees were found on many items in the shop, but not anywhere on the grandfather clock.

"No prints on the grandfather clock?" the chief of detectives mused. "That's a dead giveaway. We have our killer."

Whodunit? And how did the police know?

Solution on page 303

The Pretenders' Ball, IV

For three years running, the rebels had struck during the Grand Duchy's annual costume ball. Yet even after two assassinations and a disastrous fire, the prime minister felt obligated not to cancel.

The event was held at the old venue, the ducal palace, and, in honor of the past tragedies, the theme was black, with every costume required to have at least an accent of black.

The guests arrived and submitted themselves to the usual, useless search. The Arabian sheik gave up his scimitar and the peasant relinquished his pitchfork at the door. Dracula was allowed to keep his pointy teeth, while the Gypsy got to carry her tambourine—as long as she didn't play it.

The prime minister (Egyptian pharaoh) put on a brave front, but he knew it was just a matter of time. At a few minutes past midnight he strolled into the blue room. The first thing he noticed was a drapery tie missing from one of the curtains. He

was about to ring for a servant when he stumbled over the body of a black chess king, also known as General Fortescu, stabbed with a sword taken from the royal coat of arms above the fireplace.

There was something in the general's hand. The prime minister tried to remove it, but it was clutched tight—a piece of black fabric two inches wide and about 18 inches long, stained red with the general's blood.

The assassination took no one by surprise, and they all lined up for their usual post-crime inspection. "No one seems to be missing any parts of their costume," said the sheik (Colonel Asbek) as he scratched the blue band around his Arabian headgear.

"Well, that swatch must have come from somewhere," said the Gypsy (royal hairdresser), adjusting the black sash around her ample midriff.

Everyone was looking to the prime minister to solve this crime, just like the others. But it was the peasant (new chief of police) who quickly pointed out the assassin.

Whodunit? And how did the chief know?

Solution on page 333

Driven to Suicide

Star Cars had seemed like a great idea. Beau and Irving Plimpton would translate their passion into a business. The brothers would rent out vintage automobiles to Los Angeles film companies and production houses for background and atmosphere. Beau took care of the contracts and customers while Irving kept the cars in pristine shape, refusing to even drive them on the street.

But the Plimpton boys hadn't had a rental in weeks and were facing bankruptcy. One afternoon, an attendant spotted Beau's sports car driving into the basement garage at Beau's apartment building. An hour later, Beau's live-in girlfriend drove in and found his car occupying her spot. Peering through the dark tinted glass, Pauline could see her fiancé's hulking silhouette squeezed inside. She opened the driver's door. There, strapped into his safety belt was the body of Beau Plimpton. He'd been shot once in the left temple, the

243

revolver still in his left hand. An apparent suicide.

"Miss Pauline's spot is behind a pillar, so I didn't see anything," the attendant testified. "Didn't hear a shot either. And I was in the garage all day. Of course, if his windows were rolled up, that might account for it. Those tiny German sports cars are really well-insulated."

When the police visited the Star Cars garage, they found Irving patching a small dent in the side of their prized '48 DeSoto. "What can I do for you?" he asked the officers.

At first Irving didn't seem to understand. "Suicide? No. Beau would never kill himself. It must be Pauline—a gold digger if there ever was one. I don't know how much he's lent her. I finally talked him into trying to get the money back. And now, suddenly he's dead."

Pauline was more willing to accept suicide. "Yes, Beau was left-handed. And he had been depressed a lot lately. Do you have any reason to suspect foul play?"

The detective nodded. "Given the circumstances, suicide was virtually impossible. And we have a good idea who it was."

Even Hypochondriacs Die

"The trouble with hypochondriacs is you never know when they're sick." Such were the thoughts running through Ethel Evans's mind as she dialed the two cellular numbers, one for Dr. Mills and the other for her brother, Bertie. "Come immediately," she told them both. "Daddy just took a turn for the worse."

The hypochondriac in question, J. P. Evans, began the morning feeling well. Dr. Mills had been there for his daily examination, leaving the usual row of pills at JP's bedside. Bertie fed his father breakfast, then left for his regular day at the horse track. At 11 A.M. Ethel fed JP the first batch of pills. It was shortly after that when he began gasping for air and Ethel made her calls.

Ethel hung up and listened to the wail of a freighter as it chugged by. That was the problem with living on a residential island. Even though they were connected to the rest of the city by a

247

drawbridge, there were times when she felt so isolated.

Dr. Mills arrived in ten minutes. "I was making my rounds at the city hospital when you called. I broke every speed limit. How is he?"

"Doing better," Ethel replied. But her diagnosis proved inaccurate. Despite Dr. Mills's best efforts, J. P. Evans died a short while later, just as his only son was driving up.

As usual, Bertie had an excuse for being late. "I was on my way here when you called. I had a premonition he might get worse. I was just approaching the drawbridge and then the dang thing went up for a freighter. I had to wait there forever."

There was no up drawbridge to stop the police from arriving. And there was nothing stopping the medical examiner from coming back with a finding of death by poison.

"We don't know how it was administered," a homicide sergeant complained. "And without knowing that, we can't know who killed him."

His partner loved to contradict. "Well, I know who killed him," he said. "And that tells me how the poison was administered."

Whodunit? And what made the detective suspicious?

Solution on page 314

The Penguin House Murder

At 10 A.M. exactly, the gates to the zoo were flung open. A handful of the early visitors headed directly for the penguin house. The kids raced in to get the best view of the glass-enclosed habitat and nearly stumbled over the corpse. It was Cheryl Hammaker, a zoo employee, dressed for work and wearing a plastic feeding apron. She'd been strangled.

The medical examiner took the body's temperature, leading him to estimate that she'd been dead for well over 12 hours. "Makes sense," the zoo director said. "The penguins are fed three times a day: when the handlers get here at eight, then at noon, and finally around six, right after we close." He checked the victim's feeding apron, still filled with small fish.

"That's probably when it happened," a detec-

tive agreed as he sniffed, smelling just the faintest fishy odor. "Right before last night's feeding."

Cheryl had been a conscientious worker, arriving early and leaving late. She lived close to the zoo and kept to herself. "I'd just promoted her to department head," the director said. "With her own set of keys. Two other people were up for the job. They got pretty upset."

One of the rejected employees was Sean. "I took yesterday off," Sean testified. "My church held an all-day retreat and we didn't get home until midnight. I went right to bed. I had to be here at work by eight."

Juan, the other suspect, was found in the penguin food freezer, taking inventory of a fish delivery. "When I left last night, Cheryl was just filling up her apron for the last feeding. She told me I could go home. This morning Bert and I drove in together and went right to work in Reptile World—until we heard the news. Horrible!"

The medical examiner walked past the body again, sniffed the air, then turned to the detective. "There's something odd here," he said. "We need to question one of our suspects more thoroughly."

The Flat Motorist

"All right, Mr. Darden." The Automobile Club operator read back the information. "Your car has a flat. You have a spare, but it's in your trunk and the trunk lock is broken. You're pulled over on Route 5. I'll have a tow truck out to you immediately."

Alex Darden flipped shut his cellular phone and shivered in the night air. Maybe he'd get lucky. Maybe someone would come along before the tow truck arrived.

The tow truck driver found the car easily enough. He saw the flat tire, still on the wheel, and the jack on the ground beside it. Next he saw the blood on the jack, and finally the body. Alex Darden, middle-aged businessman, had been robbed, then bludgeoned to death.

As luck would have it, the highway patrol had been conducting a sobriety check half a mile west of the murder scene. One of the officers had taken

255

down license numbers, and before long, the police were focusing on three motorists who had passed by before the tow truck's arrival.

Arnold Aspic's motorcycle had been stopped first. "I saw a car off the side of the road," he told them the next day. "I stopped to see if the driver needed help. He needed a spare tire and, of course, I didn't have one. I should have mentioned it to you guys at the checkpoint, but I forgot."

Nan Bigelow was next. The female trucker had driven her eighteen-wheeler right past the stranded car. "I was glancing at a map," she admitted. "I'm sure I would have noticed someone on the roadside waving for help. But I didn't see a thing."

Tom Enjerry's brand-new convertible was the last vehicle to pass by before the tow truck's arrival. "I saw the car," Tom testified. "As I drove past, I looked around for the driver, but I didn't see him."

The investigating officer reviewed his notes. "I think I know who did it. And there's an easy way to check it out."

The Clumsy Thief

Charlene Tyner was half-awake when she heard it, coming from downstairs, the sound of spilling coins. She checked the time—2 A.M.—then rolled over and went back to sleep.

In the morning, when Charlene walked into her kitchen, she immediately noticed the theft. The jar in which she kept her collection of silver dollars was completely empty. That's when she recalled the late night sound. And that's when she saw the refrigerator. It was askew, the only thing out of center in the perfectly maintained kitchen.

Charlene knelt down and reached into the narrow space between the refrigerator and the cabinet. "At least they didn't get them all," she thought as she pulled her arm out. Two silver dollars, all that was left of her prized collection. The irate housewife quickly raised the alarm.

Myrna, her sullen daughter, was the first one down. A would-be model, Myrna had already

259

worked in a few fashion shows. Most of her time she spent hanging out with her no-good boyfriend. Her room was at the top of the stairs and she slept with the door open. "Someone walked by in the dark," she volunteered. "I heard the coins spilling, too. I thought it was just an accident."

Forest Tyner emerged from the downstairs bathroom. A gangling, gaunt man, he had never been Charlene's dream husband, but he was a good father. It was only after the wedding that she discovered his habit of spending half his paycheck at the local tavern. "I came in late," he admitted, alcohol still on his breath. "I didn't want to disturb you, so I slept on the couch. I didn't wake up till a few minutes ago."

Jesse, Charlene's son, lumbered down last. Obese and lazy, Jesse's twin passions were food and video games. "I came downstairs for a snack around midnight. I could hear Myrna snoring. Dad wasn't on the couch. I went back to bed and didn't hear anything."

Charlene looked around the kitchen and her heart sank. She had just figured out who had

Welcome Back, Cutter

The homicide sergeant glanced around the bedroom. It was a far cry from the obsessive neatness of the rest of the house. There were broken fixtures, scattered furniture, and a crunchy coating of shattered picture glass covering the carpet. "Quite a fight," he muttered. On the bed lay the body of Reece Cutter, a sales rep just returned from a business trip. He'd been stabbed through with an ornamental sword torn down from the bedroom wall.

The victim's brother was contacted at work, halfway across town. Earlier in the day Broderick Cutter had picked Reece up at the airport. "As soon as we got in, Reece went up to his bedroom and unpacked everything. We talked. Then I had to get to work. My shift starts at seven. Reece's wife was coming over later. Marjorie wanted Reece to sign divorce papers, but he kept refusing. I guess she doesn't have to worry about that now."

Marjorie Cutter confirmed the appointment. "I got there around 7:30 P.M." The sergeant noted that this was a full hour after Broderick had left. "I knocked and knocked, but Reece didn't answer. I figured he was just being childish—trying to avoid me."

The last person to actually speak to the victim was the manager at Parcheesi Pizza. "Around seven, Mr. Cutter called in an order: his usual ham and pineapple. He sounded nervous, not quite himself. Billy delivered it. Billy's not in any trouble, is he?"

It was Billy who discovered the body. "The front door was unlocked," the antagonistic pizza driver testified. "I wasn't about to be stood up, especially not for ham and pineapple. Yuck! So, I went inside. At first I didn't think anyone was around. And then I saw the bedroom."

The sergeant finished examining the crime scene. He opened the closet, saw the neatly hung suits and shirts, then removed the suitcase from a shelf. It was empty and immaculate, except for a tiny shard of glass caught in a side pouch. "I think we have our killer."

The Videotaped Suspect

At first it seemed like death from natural causes. Marcus Tomby, an investigative reporter, was found slumped over his desk at the *Times*, victim of a heart attack. And then the security director from the Fordham Arms apartment building came forward.

"Mr. Tomby lived at the Fordham," he told the lieutenant in charge. "He did a lot of dangerous reporting and used to joke about being knocked off some day. When I heard about his death, I reviewed the tape from the security camera in his hallway. Look."

A fuzzy image popped up, showing a red-haired, bearded man leaving the Tomby apartment and pulling closed the door. As he walked towards the camera, he lifted his hand to his face and adjusted his ring. "That's from this morning's tape. Marcus lives alone and that isn't him."

The lieutenant immediately contacted the

Times. "Yes, Marcus was on a story," explained the editor. "He suspected Metro Carting of illegally dumping toxic waste. He said he had an inside contact and was preparing a dynamite exposé."

Armed with a blurry blow-up from the security camera, the police visited Metro Carting. "Why, that's Al Cuellar," a secretary blurted out. "He started working for us last month." The lieutenant asked if Al had any reporter friends. "He never mentioned any." Did he come in to work today? "No. He never showed up." When the police telephoned Al Cuellar's number, they found it was the same as that of a midtown bar. His address corresponded to a vacant lot.

"Put out an APB," the lieutenant barked. He checked his watch. It had been less than eight hours since the reporter's death. "Get over to Tomby's apartment. Dust the place for prints."

Two hours later, there was more bad news. All the prints, both in the apartment and on the doors, belonged to the deceased. As for the mysterious suspect, Al, he had vanished completely.

The lieutenant mulled over the evidence. "I

A Maid-Made Discovery

At some point during the small party, Hazel got tired of dealing with the guests. They all had drinks in hand and seemed perfectly content. So, the maid wandered up the grand staircase to check on the sleeping children and do a little tidying up.

As soon as Hazel walked into her employer's bedroom, her eagle eyes saw that someone had been there. Taking a towel from her apron, she eradicated the quarter-size water ring from a mahogany table. "How many times do I have to tell Ms. Grant to use a coaster?" she asked the empty air. Seconds later, a breeze from an open French window drew her outside. Young Davey's skateboard was on the balcony, right by the railing edge.

"Someone could trip and fall," Hazel said with another disapproving cluck. Instinctively, she peered over the railing and was startled to see her prophecy fulfilled. Her employer, the Broadway

star Indira Grant, lay on the flagstone walk, her beautiful neck broken but her cut-crystal water glass still in one piece in her outstretched hand.

The guests were devastated by the tragic accident. Indira's husband, George, refilled his brandy snifter twice before his hand was steady enough to dial up the police. "They'll be here in five minutes," he announced.

Brent Overton, Indira's latest costar, seemed just as inconsolable. All night he'd been drinking shot glasses of whiskey. But the tragic accident sobered him instantly.

Indira's understudy, Martina Welsh, had never held much affection for the star, especially since Indira had never once missed a performance. But now, Martina put down her beer mug and became the picture of solicitude and mourning. "Whatever we do, we mustn't ever let poor Davey know it was his skateboard that made his mother slip."

"It wasn't the skateboard," Hazel muttered darkly. "Ms. Grant was pushed over that railing. And I know who did it."

How does Hazel know it wasn't an accident?

Fooling the Foolproof Alarm

After the theft of a medieval goblet, collector Felix Cheshire became obsessed with security. He improved his alarm system by installing metallic strips on the rear of all his canvases and other art objects. He didn't even trust his two longtime assistants. His latest precaution was to carry a loaded pistol and a sword hidden inside his walking cane.

As usual, Felix began his day by ushering in his assistants and setting the alarm. He had barely entered the rear research room when the alarm sounded. Grabbing his gun and cane, Felix hobbled up to the entrance and found Tanya Garfield standing by the door, a sheepish grin on her face. "I was just going out for coffee," she apologized. "I guess my earrings set it off."

The collector checked his major possessions,

found nothing missing, then reset the alarm. He settled back into the research room and accepted a cup of tea from an earring-less Tanya. Felix had no idea for how long he'd nodded off. But suddenly Jack, his other assistant, was shaking him by the shoulders.

"It's gone," Jack shouted. "The da Vinci's gone." Jack led the way to a side gallery and pointed to the small empty frame. A razor on the floor gave mute testimony to how the priceless drawing had been removed. "I was working in the front. Tanya was in one of the middle rooms. I came in here to consult the *Iliad* codex, and . . ."

Using his cane, Felix hobbled to the front gallery and out the door. His gun set off the alarm. "Stay here," he ordered, then locked his employees in and telephoned the police.

Hours later, the two assistants were putting the distraught man to bed. "The police searched everywhere," the old collector moaned as Tanya took his cane and Jack began taking off his shoes. "The alarm was on. No one could have removed the drawing without setting it off."

The thief suppressed a smile and tried to look as

concerned as Felix's other assistant.

How could the drawing have been removed? And who is the most likely suspect?

Solution on page 316

Death in the Woods

It was a beautiful afternoon. Dr. Ben Kramer's guests were roaming his country estate, enjoying themselves—until a series of growls and screams pierced the air. Robert Kelly grabbed a rifle from the den and followed the sounds, only to find the good doctor being mauled by a bear. A shot in the air scared the animal off.

"Go get Ben's medical bag," Jorey Abrams said as he bent over their unconscious host. From Ben's half-filled basket, they could see he'd been gathering wild strawberries.

Ursula Abrams and Rebecca Kelly returned together, having found the bag in their host's bedroom. Ursula, a nurse, took over, administering a vial of smelling salts. It was no use. Seconds later, Ben Kramer convulsed and died.

The local sheriff arrived and was about to call it an accident when he found a note caught on a thorny bush not far from the attack. It looked like

a list of reminders.

"Be first to attend BK after attack. Death must look natural. Do everything to avoid autopsy. Seek quick cremation." The sheriff decided to investigate. Handwriting samples were taken from all four of the guests.

"This is ridiculous," Ursula said that evening as the two couples sat over a solemn dinner in the dead man's house. "There's no way anyone could plan a bear attack. Plus, none of us was anywhere near Ben."

The women had taken over the cooking, following the recipes Ben had laid out. "I didn't feel right about mixing his wild strawberries in the fruit tart," Rebecca sniffed. "Didn't seem right. Besides, Robert's terribly allergic." No one touched the dessert.

"Well, someone must have been out there," Jorey argued. "That note didn't appear by magic. Maybe they'll be able to match the handwriting."

But the note was written in block letters and there was no positive match. There also seemed to be no motive. The doctor had been generous to a fault, and it was actually difficult not to take advantage of him.

The police never solved this one. Can you? Who killed Dr. Kramer and how?

Solution on page 311

Murder Works Overtime

Roger Vail was having a bad day. First off, the advertising executive spilled coffee over the back of the roller chair in his redecorated office, resulting in a permanent stain. Then his computer went haywire. With his hard drive gone, Roger had to stay late to complete a report. And to top it off, while he was working late, he was shot three times in the back and killed.

When the cleaning woman entered Roger's office that night, she thought it was empty. The chair back faced her, a virtual wall of beige. Her expert eye quickly noticed the three tiny blemishes on the fabric, three little round holes. She came closer, rolling the chair away from the broken computer and toward the light. Roger Vail's corpse slumped forward, the holes in his back matching the bullet holes pumped into the chair.

Roger's death shocked his colleagues. "Everyone liked him," Joan Jackson sighed the

next morning as she watered her flowers. "If there was a murder here, I would have expected . . ." She left it unfinished, piquing the curiosity of the interrogating officer. Blakemore Advertising, it turned out, was a hotbed of seething emotions.

Joan, for example, was having a feud with her creative partner, Elsa Gripper. Just the day before, the two of them had come to blows, resulting in Joan's dramatic black eye. And then there was Sammy Frick. On the very day of the murder, Sammy had loudly threatened to kill Orrie Kindale, the man who Sammy felt had cheated him out of a much-deserved promotion.

Orrie occupied the office right next to the victim's. He tried to make light of the company squabbles, but he was definitely nervous. "Tempers flare in the advertising world, but no one really means it." The executive rested his arm over the top of his chair, as if trying to hide the brown stain that poured down the tall chair back.

"Orrie knows more than he's saying," the homicide captain muttered. "I think I know what happened."

What does the captain think happened? Who killed Roger Vail?

Solution on page 327

Two Places at Once

All evidence pointed to Frank Fortini. "He has motive," the homicide chief told his men. "Frank's Uncle Gregor, the victim, just won the state lottery. Frank and his brothers are Gregor's only relatives and would inherit the $14 million prize.

"Also, Frank had opportunity. Gregor was a paranoid guy living in an isolated cabin. He always kept his doors locked and hated strangers. Since there was no forced entry and no sign of a struggle, we know Gregor was attacked by someone he knew and trusted.

"To top it off, we found direct evidence at the cabin. There were fresh tire tracks, perfectly matching the tires from Frank's mountain bike. And . . ." The chief was getting angry. "And we found a ticket from today's lottery near the scene—with Frank's prints on it.

"The only trouble is . . ." The chief pounded the table. "He has an alibi. On the night Gregor

was killed, Frank was breaking into Avalon Hardware. Normally there'd be nothing to steal. But the store manager neglected to take the day's receipts to the bank. An alert patrolman looked through a window and saw Frank prying open the cash register. The coroner says Gregor was killed at the same time Frank was being read his rights."

"Frank's a petty robber," Jake Fortini later told the police in his brother's defense. "He'd steal the pennies from your loafers, you could count on it. But he'd never kill."

Frank's other brother was a teller at Avalon's only bank. "I saw Frank right after I got off work," said Emil Fortini. "We had a couple drinks. Frank seemed a little hard up for money, but that was normal."

Frank had little to say in his own defense. "I keep my bike in an unlocked garage. Anyone could have used it. As for my uncle, I haven't been up to his cabin in a week."

The homicide chief scratched his head. "I don't have any hard evidence. But I have a pretty good idea who did it and how the mur-

Dead-End Stoolie

It was a cloudy Sunday, with the skies threatening rain all morning and showers anticipated in the afternoon. So Detective Wilson didn't really mind when he was called in to work.

A tourist had gotten himself lost in an industrial section of town. At the very end of a dead-end alley, the poor visitor came across the body of Vinny the Fish, a stoolie who'd been supplying Detective Wilson with information on several ongoing mob investigations.

"Both kneecaps busted," the on-scene officer said as he pointed to the corpse crumpled up against the blank wall. "Chest cavity was crushed in, too. We'll know more when the medical examiner arrives."

Wilson didn't wait for the M.E. Instead, he looked up the addresses of three of Vinny's associates and drove off to see them. Someone had found out about Vinny's cooperation. Wilson felt

he owed it to the stoolie to find his killer.

Gummy Moran was on the street in front of his modest brick row house, washing his car. Gummy shrugged off the news of Vinny's death and kept chewing his ever-present wad of gum. "He probably got mugged. Don't waste your time on this loser. Go back to catching mobsters." And he laughed.

Wilson found his second suspect at the clubhouse the mob had built for the neighborhood baseball diamond. Ricky Fricker was in the equipment room, checking bats for cracks and oiling gloves. "It's volunteer work," he said smugly. "You should try it. Look, I'm sorry about poor Vinny, but I barely knew the guy."

Sean Monahan was a little harder to find, but Wilson eventually tracked him to the Oak Shillelagh, an Irish restaurant. "My sources tell me old Vinny bought the farm," he said as soon as Wilson walked in. Wilson knew all about Monahan's sources, some of whom were probably inside Wilson's department. "Why are you wasting time on Vinny's death. Was he stooling for you?"

"Don't worry about my time. I know how to

concentrate my energies. There's only one suspect I'm really interested in."

Whom does Wilson suspect? And why?

Solution on page 310

A Lapse in Security

Preparations were all in place for the Peace Treaty Summit. Nary a twig was out of place in the secluded, wooded retreat. The service staff had been cleared by security. And the entire compound was off-limits to motor vehicles until the dignitaries started arriving in their limousines.

Security Chief Derrick Gerber was making a final tour on his bicycle. What if an assassin had somehow managed to get in? Gerber's suspicious mind focused on one of the newly hired staff. He decided to run another check.

An hour later, Gerber's body was discovered in a ravine. Gil Abel, the security chief's assistant, was immediately notified.

Abel cycled up the main road, noting with irritation a shaggy black piece of bloody roadkill along the shoulder, being toyed with by a kitchen cat. Twenty yards later, he was at the ravine. Gerber had put up quite a struggle before suc-

cumbing to a flurry of stab wounds. "I've had my own suspicions," Abel mumbled to himself. "I suppose it's time to check them out."

Pearl Weimar, head chef, had been hired by special request of the French delegate. "I've been here in the kitchen all morning," she told Abel as she sharpened knives on a whetstone. "You'll probably find out: At the last conference I worked, there was an assassination. Unsolved." Abel knew this. That's why she was on his list.

Abel located Edgar Vichy, director of protocol, in his room. Edgar seated the security chief out of view of the two empty wig stands on the dresser. "He doesn't want me to know," Abel thought with amusement as he gazed at the dark, obvious toupee mounted on the fussy little man's head.

Edgar claimed to have been taking a walk. "I was on the far side of the compound. I didn't hear or see a thing."

The third suspect was Avril Alsace, the groundskeeper. "I was by the south fence, raking pine needles by the conference center. I saw Gerber cycling by. He waved and circled the building, but he didn't stop."

Whodunit? And what piece of evidence implicates the killer?

Solution on page 322

Alibi at Sea

During a storm at sea, millionaire art lover C. Michael Ekshun popped out on the deck of his luxurious yacht. He didn't hear a thing as his killer sneaked up behind him, brandishing a deadly sharp letter opener. Moments after the murder, his body was pushed overboard, disappearing into the swirling foam.

When the skies cleared and the yacht pulled into harbor, police questioned the three surviving passengers: Michael's stylishly dressed wife, Sprinkle Ekshun; his secretary, Morey Fishant; and a shifty-eyed art dealer named Count Yuri Ceets. Each suspect had an alibi.

"I was in the lounge, doing my nails," Sprinkle told them. The widow stuffed her hands into the pockets of her Dior dressing gown. The police immediately noticed a wet patch on her robe front. In the middle of the wet patch was a stubborn red stain that had refused to come out.

298

299

"I was in my cabin writing," Count Yuri said as he showed the police a neatly written five-page letter, all in Russian. "To my dear mother, the Countess," he explained. A translation of the letter proved that Yuri had indeed written to his mother—a cleaning lady living in Bensonhurst.

Morey, the secretary, claimed to be opening correspondence in the yacht's office at the time of the murder. The envelopes were all torn open. "I couldn't find the letter opener," he said with an embarrassed shrug. The police noticed a fresh gash on Morey's right wrist. "This happened when I stumbled. I cut myself on one of Mr. Ekshun's glass sculptures."

The police haven't yet investigated motive, but already they see that one of the three alibis doesn't hold water—as opposed to Michael, who is holding several gallons by the time they fish him out of the Atlantic.

Whodunit?

Solution on page 302

WHODUNIT SOLUTIONS

Solutions appear in alphabetical order by story title.

Agent Brown's Shining Moment

When Agent Brown got into the Cadillac, he had to adjust the rearview mirror. This meant that the previous driver had been significantly different in height. Since the shorter mobster was close to Brown's own height, he knew the taller man had to be the driver. Therefore, the shorter man was the shooter.

Airport Insecurity

Chief Moretti had been momentarily puzzled by Johnny's schedule. It was already after 4 P.M., and yet when Johnny checked his watch he talked about trying to make a 4 o'clock meeting "way up in the Bronx."

Then Moretti recalled a simple fact: Chicago is

in a different time zone, one hour earlier. If Johnny's watch was set on Chicago time, such a nervous mistake would have been understandable.

Moretti looked at Johnny's watch and saw that it was indeed an hour behind. "If I'm not mistaken, this watch belonged to our murdered visitor. Let's check it out."

Alibi at Sea

Count Yuri Ceets. No one could have written a neat, five-page letter during a storm at sea. Yuri had obviously written the letter earlier and was using it as an alibi.

Sprinkle's alibi is plausible. If she had been trying to do her nails during a storm, the polish might have spilled, leaving the red stain on her robe. Plus, her manicure might have turned out so badly that she would try to hide her hands.

There is also nothing wrong with Morey's alibi. The gash on his wrist could have been the result of an accident caused by the violent rocking of the boat. As for the missing letter opener, anyone could have walked into the office and stolen it.

Yuri eventually confessed. He had been selling the millionaire forged paintings. Ekshun had grown suspicious. As soon as they reached port, he was going to have the paintings examined by an independent expert.

Archie's Christmas Surprise

Gene Granger supposedly did not hear about the suicide until he arrived on the nineteenth floor. And yet, when Granger unlocked the door to his conference room, there was no Christmas present waiting under the tree for Archie. Granger had personally selected presents for all of his employees—all except the man he killed, the man he knew would be dead. There was no other way to explain the oversight.

Hank notified the police, who soon uncovered Granger's massive embezzlement.

Around-the-Clock Murder

Since Jules Marigold wound the grandfather clock shortly before closing, the lack of fingerprints on the clock indicates that someone wiped it clean. The only reason for doing this would be to eliminate a key piece of evidence. So, why would the killer need to wipe his prints off the clock?

The police deduced that the murder did not occur at 11:09, but earlier. After the murder, the killer turned the hands forward to 11:09, wiped his fingerprints off, then purposely knocked over the clock. All the police had to do was find the one suspect with an ironclad alibi for 11:09 P.M.: Charlie Weed.

An Attack of Gas

The dead flies on the windowsill were solid evidence that Gerald Espy's room had been gassed after sunrise. If it had been done during the dark of night, the flies would not have congregated by the light of the east-facing window.

Only one of the suspects has a morning alibi—Frank Townly, who had been locked inside the tavern. That means it was Melvin who had sneaked into his father's room that morning and committed the murderous act.

The Bad Samaritan

There was no attacker. Stan had killed his partner, hidden the payroll bag off the side of the road, then shot himself in the shoulder to add believability.

The hole in Stan's story lay in his description. If the two men were checking the engine, then the car's hood would have been up, and Stan would not have been able to see them standing "right in front" of the car. He also wouldn't have been able to see the killer pull the gun from his jacket. And he certainly wouldn't have been able to drive off, not with the hood still up.

The Brothers Ilirium

The choir testified that Mike had been thrown before impact. And yet blood had been found in the car, indicating that Mike had been dead or injured before being thrown. The only person who testified to having actually seen Mike drive off was Roger, making him the prime suspect.

"We had a fight out in the garage," Roger confessed.

"I knocked him down and he hit his head. It was an accident, but I was scared. I put the body in the convertible and drove down to the first sharp turn and stopped the car. Then I put a rock on the gas pedal and switched it into gear. I didn't worry about the blood because I didn't think he'd be thrown."

Bye-Bye, Bully

Blake Fromm claimed to have been outdoors all morning, painting the porch ceiling, a messy job if there ever was one. And yet his jeans were nearly spotless.

The most logical explanation for this oddity is that Blake went inside toward the end of his painting job, changed his clothes, then came out again to finish. Why would he do that? Because his original shirt and trousers were covered in blood—Pete Weider's blood.

Chili con Carnage

Winston resorted to murder in order to take Gil's place. That was also the reason behind stuffing him into the chili pot: to prevent anyone from salvaging Gil's dinner after he died.

Winston had counted on the murder being discovered early that morning. The late discovery fouled up his plans. In order to prepare homemade chili, one needs to soak pinto beans for at least eight hours. Winston had to start soaking the beans that morning, before the body was actually found, or else they wouldn't be ready. Unfortunately for him, the Austin police commissioner was a chili aficionado and noticed the discrepancy.

A Chinese Lie Detector

At dawn the next day, the emperor's court returned to the public garden and were amazed to find that not one but *two* of the bamboo stalks were higher. "Were there two thieves?" the captain wondered out loud.

"No, just one" the wizard replied. "Arrest the man with the short stalk. He was the only one with a reason to fear my magic. Thinking that his own stalk would grow, he sneaked back here in the middle of the night and cut it a finger joint shorter."

The Clumsy Thief

The askew refrigerator was the pivotal clue. It showed that the thief had reached into the narrow space in order to retrieve the spilled coins. The fact that the thief didn't reach back far enough to find the last two coins pointed Charlene to an inevitable conclusion. The thief's arm was thicker than her own.

Daughter Myrna was a thin model. Husband Forest was gangling and gaunt. But Jesse was obese. Only he would have been unable to reach the last two coins.

The Coach's Last Play

Coach Bricker survived long enough to try to identify his attacker. The only problem was that, lying in the middle of a football field, he didn't have access to pencil or paper. All he had was his paperback novel. Thinking quickly, Bricker tore out the book's last page and kept it clutched in his hand. His killer would be identified by the last words on that page, "THE END."

The Convent Mystery

Since nothing was ever missing, the inspector theorized that the intruder might be trying to remove something that arrived over the weekend. The only thing that regularly arrived over the weekend was the mail. His theory was bolstered by the fact that the Saturday mail was the only delivery personally handled by Mother Superior—each Monday morning.

The one woman who might benefit from intercepting the mail was Barbara, who had lied on her application. She never worked for an Alaskan convent. During the week, Barbara screened the letters, looking for an Alaskan postmark. Then every Saturday, she broke in shortly after the mail delivery and checked again.

Dead-End Stoolie

The stoolie had been found against the wall of a lonely, dead-end alley. Detective Wilson left the crime scene before the murder weapon had been determined. But the unusual behavior of one of his suspects led him to a theory of how Vinny met his death.

It had been threatening rain all day. And yet when Wilson approached Gummy Moran, the mobster was washing his car. No one washes his car when rain is expected—not unless he wants to remove evidence of a vehicular homicide.

Death by Chocolate

One thing had been missing from the victim's room, his custom-made bake-off apron. The detective soon found the apron, however—on Kelly Yeagar's body. The apron Kelly had worn earlier only came down to her knees. This one came down to her calves.

While bludgeoning her lanky victim in his sleep, Kelly had accidentally splattered her own apron with blood. Since she couldn't possibly wear it again, Kelly stole Bullock's longer apron and disposed of her own.

Death in the Woods

Once it's realized that the note in the woods belonged to Ben, the crime becomes less mysterious. The initials don't stand for Ben Kramer but Bob Kelly.

Dr. Kramer had been intending to kill Bob Kelly by feeding his friend a tart filled with wild strawberries. Then, when Bob had an allergic attack, the doctor was planning to "revive" him with the poisoned smelling salts. Death would be blamed on the fruit. Ben was unwittingly killed by the murder weapon he had prepared for someone else.

Death of a Deceiver

The naked body on the autopsy table held the pivotal clue. On Jerry Fisher's ring finger was a tan line, just where his wedding ring had been.

Lieutenant Miller pointed it out. "When Jerry went over to Gail's apartment, he naturally removed his wedding ring. Unfortunately, he forgot about the tan line. It's winter here, so he never had to deal with this problem before. There's no way Gail could have spent the afternoon with him and not noticed that line."

His partner nodded. "Let's go back and talk to Ms. Lowenski."

The Dirty Cop

Officer Brady had observed his suspects well. Marjorie, for example, was right-handed, as indicated by the watch on her left wrist. Adam's use of his right hand to zip up his trousers indicated the same thing. On the other hand—literally—was Charlie Salt, who had been writing with his left.

Since a left-handed person naturally tears off matches from the left side of a matchbook, Officer Brady knew that Charlie was his dirty cop.

Driven to Suicide

It would have been impossible for a large man in a small car to shoot himself in the left temple, not with his safety belt on and the window rolled up. There wouldn't be enough elbow room. Beau must have been murdered elsewhere, then driven to the apartment building garage.

Irving always kept the vintage cars in mint condition. But when the police came, he was fixing a dent—even though the car hadn't been driven in weeks. The police noticed this and theorized that the car had been dented during a fight, a fatal fight in which Irving killed his brother.

The Emery Emerald

On the surface, the robbery appeared puzzling. Why would the thief go to the trouble of stealing dozens of gems merely to discard all but one? Mrs. Emery could only think of one logical reason. The thief was color-blind and had to scoop up all of them. Later on, his accomplice identified the emerald and they threw out the rest.

From Klaus Braun's appearance that day at the exhibition, Mrs. Emery had good cause to believe that he had trouble distinguishing colors.

Even Hypochondriacs Die

Right after making the phone calls, Ethel heard a freighter chug by the island. This was confirmed by Bertie, who was delayed by the raised draw-bridge. And yet Dr. Mills seemed to have no problem with the drawbridge. Why? Because he was already on the island, not at the city hospital.

It was Dr. Mills who poisoned the pills. Knowing approximately when the symptoms would take effect, the doctor made sure he was somewhere nearby. He wanted to be the first on the scene, just in case something went wrong. When it looked like JP might recover from the poison, Dr. Mills administered an extra dose.

Eye Spy

It's a cold winter's day, and Lu Ching's apartment is almost as chilly. So, why is the desk fan whirling? And in an empty apartment?

Julia turned off the fan and found the eight negatives. They were taped to the four fan blades, one on each side of each blade. The speed of the fan's rotation had rendered them invisible to the naked eye.

The Flat Motorist

The murder weapon, a jack, could not have come from the victim's car, since his trunk lock was broken. It was most likely the property of the killer, who pretended to be coming to the aid of the stranded motorist before crushing in his head with the tool.

An eighteen-wheeler and a motorcycle would not be equipped with car jacks. But a brand-new convertible would. The police checked the trunk of Tom Enjerry's car. They found the standard spare tire, but no jack. It didn't take long for the police to confirm that the murder weapon had come from Enjerry's trunk.

Fooling the Foolproof Alarm

After the first alarm, Felix checked his major possessions. The da Vinci was still there. The only other time the drawing could have been removed was during the second alarm, the one Felix personally set off. Felix himself could have unwittingly carried out the da Vinci—rolled up and wrapped around the sword inside his hollow cane.

The most likely suspect would be Tanya, who (a) gave him the cup of tea that lulled him to sleep and (b) took possession of the cane as they were putting him to bed. She would have plenty of time to remove the painting from the cane after Felix went to bed.

Friends at the Office

By examining Wiley's ashtray, Gilson concluded that the lawyer had been a smoker and that he lit his cigarettes with matches. The cheap lighter on the floor by the body had probably been left accidentally—by Wiley's killer.

Jackson Cod smoked cigars but didn't seem to

have a lighter or matches in his studio with him. That made him a prime suspect.

Good-Neighbor Policy

Jake had made his tour of the property in the driving rain. And yet the carpet under the open window was dry except for the muddy footprints. This meant that the window hadn't been broken until later, after Millie had gone back to bed. It also meant that the burglar was already in the house. Otherwise, Shamus would have started barking again.

Jimmy eventually confessed. He had used his keys to get inside. When Shamus started barking, Jimmy hid, waiting until Jake left and the lights went out in Millie's house. Then he stole the earrings and set up the scene to implicate Jake.

The Gypsy Thief

Carmen was on the right track when she said that the thief would have had to be very stealthy. All three suspects wore jangling ornaments (spurs, a bracelet, and earrings) that might easily have awakened the others.

The giveaway was Dahlia's bracelet. When she settled down to sleep, it was on her right wrist. When she got up, it was on her left. She had obviously removed it during the nap period. Why? In order to more silently sneak over to Marco and steal his purse.

Hand in the Cookie Jar

The blond hair, the bottles, and the caps are red herrings. All they show is that Morton and Victor shared a pair of late-night beers. The vital clue is the out-of-place chair by the kitchen counter.

Six-foot-tall Valerie didn't need a chair to reach the cookie jar. Neither would her twin brother nor a professional basketball player. But Glenda, described as dumpy, was well under six feet. She was the only one who would need help in order to reach the jar.

A Hard Day's Night

When the police arrived on the scene, they did not know whether Clive Custard had been leaving the house or had just arrived home. At 8:30 A.M., the odds were that he was locking up, on his way to work. The parcel delivery driver, however, seemed to know for a fact that the young businessman had just come home—something he could only know if he'd been there himself.

High-Rise Homicide

Even though the knife had severed an artery, there was only one isolated pool of blood. So, how did the victim get 15 feet away from the telephone base without leaving a blood trail? He didn't. Someone placed the receiver in the dead man's hand, someone who needed an alibi.

The police concentrated on the suspect with the alibi. Alex Torful eventually confessed. He had killed Xavier in a fight over business. Alex put the phone receiver in Xavier's hand, then went to his own apartment to change his bloody clothes.

After leaving the building via the fire exit, Alex called the doorman from a pay phone, pretending to be the victim. When he walked into the building seconds later, he assumed he had a perfect alibi.

A Housewarming Theft

None of the suspects has an ironclad alibi, but the thief did accidentally leave behind a clue, the piece of black plastic tape used to hold open the kitchen door latch.

Since the burglary had been a crime of opportunity, the burglar must have had the tape on him during the previous work day. A painter might have used edging tape. A plumber might have used putty or a sealant. But the most likely person to have black plastic tape—also known as electrician's tape—would have been Ed the electrician.

An Inside Job

The partners' meeting was held every Friday without fail at 1 P.M. And yet, on this particular afternoon, it was well after one and Betty, the executive secretary, was still setting up the conference table. Betty had obviously known that Arthur Klein would not be making his regular train. She knew because she herself had arranged the robbery, informing her brother-in-law of her boss's arrival time at Grand Central Station and the valuable bonds he would be carrying.

The Kidnapping Killer

Fernando, the janitor. Blood stops flowing shortly after death. If Alice's body had been moved an hour and a half after her murder, there would have been no large bloodstain in the elevator. The blood proves that Alice had been moved from her apartment to the basement shortly after death and that Fernando must be involved.

Fernando eventually admitted to being paid off by Dale, the ex-boyfriend, to assist him in covering up Alice's murder. It had been a crime of passion, and the ransom note was a feeble attempt to throw off the police.

Killer Camp Food

Richie. The youngest Tafel brother claimed to have eaten a huge portion of blueberry cobbler. And yet, minutes later, without having had a chance to brush his teeth, Richie was flashing a dazzlingly white smile. If he'd really eaten cooked blueberries, his teeth would have been stained.

As they prepared dinner that evening, Richie poisoned the cobbler, knowing that his uncle would be the first at the dessert pot. After observing his uncle take his usual large portion, Richie dished out the rest for himself, then disposed of it in the woods.

A Lapse in Security

Two oddities caught Abel's attention: (1) Nary a twig was out of place in the wooded compound, and there was no vehicular traffic. So, how does one account for the shaggy, bloody piece of roadkill? And (2) why were both of Edgar's wig stands empty?

Abel went back to the road just in time to stop the cat from demolishing the blood-covered toupee.

Edgar Vichy was the assassin. During his struggle with Gerber, the victim tore off Edgar's wig. Since Edgar could no longer wear the bloody toupee, he disposed of it in the woods. It had been dragged up to the road by a roaming cat.

The Last Poker Hand

Had Bugsy, with his dying efforts, been trying to identify his attacker? If his killer had been the Reverend King, he might have picked a king from the scattered cards. Holding a jack would have fingered Jack Lawrence. Any spade would have identified Alan Spade. And all the dying man had to do to identify Joseph Blush was to grab the empty bottle of Blush gin. Instead of any of these clues, however, the victim was holding five diamonds, otherwise known as a flush.

When Jack Lawrence mentioned the other players, he got one name wrong. Instantly, the sergeant knew the truth. Jack had killed Bugsy, then placed the cards in his hand, hoping to frame the man he had mistakenly known as "Joe Flush."

The Locked Room

Sheila testified that Jack looked through the keyhole. According to Jack, however, he made the suggestion but didn't have a chance to act on it before his brothers started ramming the door. Sheila may have been in a position to hear Jack talk about keyhole spying, but she didn't actually see him do it.

The most likely place for Sheila to have heard Jack was from inside the bedroom itself. Sheila killed her mother, set up the suicide, then hid behind the door. After the boys broke it in, she emerged from hiding, making it look as if she'd just arrived.

Long-Distance Murder

The homicide captain was struck by the fact that the study extension phone held no fingerprints, even though the victim had used the instrument just minutes before. The only reason the killer would wipe off the telephone was if he or she had used it. This led to the arrest of

Jim and Melba Cord.

Jim Cord wasn't at home 30 miles away. He was right inside the family mansion, strangling his father. When his wife shouted for him to pick up the phone, Jim heard her voice over the nurse's speakerphone. He picked up the extension in the mansion study, thereby establishing his alibi. Afterwards, he wiped off the phone and left by the French doors, the same way he'd entered.

Looking for a Lookout

The homeless alcoholic was obviously faking his drunken state. Since alcohol doesn't freeze, his bourbon bottle must have been filled with colored water. So, why would a sober person be out on such a cold night pretending to be drunk? He had to be the lookout.

A Maid-Made Discovery

If Indira had tripped on the skateboard, it would not have wound up right by the railing. It would have been pushed backwards.

Unfortunately, Hazel accidentally destroyed the most telling piece of evidence, the water ring on the table. The offending glass had been the size of a quarter, much too small for a crystal water glass, a brandy snifter, or a beer mug. It's just the right size for a shot glass, however. The killer had to be Brent Overton.

Maria's Last Clue

Sergeant Vacca considered Maria's final moments. Dazed and dying, she had dragged herself across the floor to her computer. She reached up to the keyboard and, using her touch-typing skills, identified her attacker. But what if she had accidentally placed her fingers on the wrong row of keys?

The sergeant performed an experiment, placing his fingers one row above where they should be. He then closed his eyes and typed out the names of his three suspects. Within seconds he had a match. "48dy 28oo8qjw" equaled "Rich Williams."

Murder Works Overtime

The victim had not been killed in his own chair. That fact, combined with the chair's high-backed design and Vail's broken computer, led the captain to the following theory.

Vail stayed late. Since his computer was broken, he had to finish his report on Orrie Kindale's computer. When the killer entered Kindale's office, he fired through the chair back without getting a clear view of his victim. After realizing he'd shot the wrong man, the killer rolled the corpse into Vail's office and replaced the bullet-riddled chair with Vail's coffee-stained duplicate.

Kindale also noticed the chair exchange and came to the same conclusion: The killer was probably his enemy, Sammy Frick.

Myra's Three Sons

Sherman and Donald could both be telling the truth. Donald could have arrived after Sherman and not realized his brother was already in the cottage. But Luther is most decidedly lying. He

327

could not have turned on the electricity and then made himself a cocktail with ice from the refrigerator's ice tray. He must have arrived at least several hours after Sherman switched on the power.

The inspector knew that Luther must have made the cocktail in an attempt to calm his nerves—after murdering his own mother.

A Nun Too Pretty Murder

When Sister Margaret Mary gulped and her starched collar bobbed up and down, Special Agent McCormack knew he had his man—literally. The bobbing collar indicated the hidden existence of an Adam's apple. Only men have prominent Adam's apples. Harriet Murmer had been killed by a hit man disguised as a nun.

The deteriorated body of the real Sister Margaret Mary was found the next day, floating in the Hudson River.

The Nutty Strangler

Anyone who has ever eaten red pistachio nuts knows that the dye from the shells comes off easily and can stain. The sergeant suspects the man with the broken-down car. He thinks the man saw the officers coming and started working under the hood in order to hide the red dye. If the police carefully wipe his hands, they should be able to find traces of the telltale dye underneath the grease.

The Party's Over

The captain noticed that Fernando's balloons had been on the lawn, indicating that they had been blown up with regular air, not helium. And yet, on a windless day, there was one balloon stuck high in a tree. The captain could only conclude that Fernando had planted it there. When Fernando climbed the tree and glanced over the fence, he saw no evidence of a robbery. He actually committed the crime later, while his friend went down the street to place the 911 call.

The Penguin House Murder

If Cheryl's body had been lying around for 12 to 16 hours, the fish in her apron would have been giving off much more than just a faint fishy odor. They would have stunk.

The medical examiner deduced that someone cooled the body artificially, trying to confuse him about the time of death. Cheryl must have been killed much later, perhaps just an hour or two ago. The killer then placed the body in the penguin food freezer until shortly before the zoo opened. The police should concentrate on the suspect who had an ironclad alibi last night, but no alibi this morning—Sean.

The Piney Bluffers

Although two of the stories may sound suspicious, they are really perfectly plausible. Al Fishburn's story, however, contained a definite falsehood. Al said that he and his partner had set up their tent in the morning. And yet, the ground inside the tent was wet, indicating that they had set it up either during the rainstorm or after. The officer detained them for further questioning.

The Playboy's Empty Vase

The presence of broken glass on the terrace shows that the windowpane of the French door had been broken from inside the house, not outside. At the time of the theft, only one person was actually inside. When the police finally realized the significance of the glass shards, they concentrated on Gene and soon discovered the diamond cufflinks hidden in the valet's sock drawer.

Postgraduate Murder

The noise that Glen heard out back supports Sonny's story of coming home a few minutes before the murder and tripping over something. The torn-out extension cord and the bent prong also support Sonny's story. But, if Sonny's fall pulled the cord out of the outlet, then Bill Mayer would have found himself suddenly in the dark.

Why didn't Bill mention the failure of his work light? Simple—he didn't know about it. At that moment, he was already sneaking upstairs, intent on shooting Harry Harris, the friend who had seduced his girl.

The Pretenders' Ball

When the pirate arrived, he was wearing a fake peg leg, with his real leg tucked up under his pantaloons. Shortly after the murder, however, he was standing on two good legs, as evidenced by his ability to run and take the steps two at a time.

The prime minister noticed the change and was clever enough to piece it together. The provincial mayor, a rebel sympathizer, had used the wooden leg to bludgeon the old duke to death. He then threw the crucial piece of evidence over the balcony into the chasm.

The Pretenders' Ball, II

The prime minister knew there was one sure way to start a fire inside a locked building, as long as the building had a window receiving direct sunlight. A lens could be used to focus light on any highly flammable object, such as an old document. And it works through window glass. The only costumed guest who had come prepared with just such a lens was the royal stable master, Sherlock Holmes.

The Pretenders' Ball, III

When the clown arrived, he was carrying a bunch of balloons. When he was searched, however, his hands were in his pockets. What happened to the balloons?

The ever clever prime minister deduced that the clown (a disgruntled royal postal courier) had tied the light but deadly derringer to the balloons and sent it sailing into the night sky.

The Pretenders' Ball, IV

As he was being stabbed, the general reached out to his killer, grabbing part of his assailant's costume and tearing it off. After the murder, the killer couldn't take back his black costume piece. It was stained with blood. So he improvised, replacing it with a drapery tie from the curtains in the blue room.

The chief of police saw that the only costumed guest wearing a piece of blue fabric was the Arabian sheik.

The Pre-Valentine's Day Murder

If the crime had occurred on Valentine's Day or after, there would be several possibilities. But since it happened on the day before, it's safe to assume that this man who "had absolutely nothing" stole both the candy and the watch. On examining the crease on the watch strap, the police determined that it belonged to a man with a narrower wrist. Peter Peaver was the only student to fit that description.

Peter had been planning to send the poisoned chocolates to a girl who had spurned his advances—until Gilly sneaked into his apartment and carried out his deadly theft.

A Quali-Tee Theft

Mark Price. The thief had mere minutes, and yet he knew exactly where to go in the crowded shop and what to take, including unpriced coins and loose diamonds from a locked file cabinet. It had to be an inside job, done by someone who knew the establishment well.

This narrows the suspects down to the employees, Mark Price and Abe Ketchum. If Abe had committed the theft, however, he wouldn't have neglected to take the emerald brooch, an item that came into the shop after Mark had already left for the day.

The Queen Glendora Photos

The row of scalloped cuts on the empty envelope indicated a pair of nail scissors. Since the thief cut open the envelope before leaving the office building, this clue pointed to the only person to carry such scissors as part of her regular equipment: the manicurist.

Dodo was arrested along with her boyfriend Bart, who had arranged the sale to *True Gossip Monthly*.

A Real False Alarm

Two facts pointed the inspector in the right direction: (a) Martha didn't hear the smashing of the car window. (b) Elliot said he looked under the front passenger seat for the necklace case, yet his prints were not there, not even on a door handle.

When the alarm went off by accident that night, Elliot seized the opportunity, smashing the window and stealing his sister's necklace. The alarm covered up the sound of breaking glass. But Elliot's big mistake lay in wiping away his prints. Sometimes fingerprints can prove you innocent.

The Shortcut Robbery

Mary Ramsey testified that she saw her assailant only from the rear. And yet she stated categorically that he had been wearing a cardigan, a sweater that buttons up the front. There was no way she could have known from the rear if the sweater was a pullover or a cardigan. Mary was lying.

The police soon discovered that she faked her own attack in order to steal the jewelry store's receipts.

The Smuggler and the Clever Wife

The guard's wife caught the one discrepancy no one else did. The Mercedes woman had used a different-colored car, not black this time, but dark blue. Could the woman be driving a different car on each trip across the border? It was worth checking out.

Late that same afternoon, when passport control stopped the woman from re-entering the U.S., they found her dressed much more casually. They also found her taking the bus. It was so simple that no one had seen it. The woman was smuggling cars—a whole fleet of stolen Mercedes.

The Stolen Cleopatra

The fact that both men wanted to be searched meant that the thief no longer had the coin on him. Since neither man had left the Marsh premises after the theft, the coin must still be there, hidden somewhere.

The patrolman noticed that the plants had not been watered. He also noticed that the potted

337

plant was leaning toward the darkened living room instead of the sunny kitchen windows. Since plants naturally lean toward sunlight, the patrolman knew that someone had recently moved it. Sure enough, the ancient coin was hidden under the pot. The patrolman took Kenny Johnson in for questioning.

In Kenny's statement, he said that Digby was holding the coin after leaving the house. This was obviously a lie.

Strangulation Station

The mayor wisely eliminated the impossible. The killer had to be one of the three survivors and must have brought the murder weapon with him. The only long, strong, thin cords the mayor could see were the leather shoelaces on the bodyguard's boots.

The bodyguard, a paid assassin, had sneaked the smoke bomb and the gas mask on board. While the dictator was asleep and the others preoccupied, he put on the gas mask and detonated the bomb. After strangling the colonel, he simply re-laced his boot, threw the gas mask into a corner, and joined his colleagues in unconsciousness.

The Suicidal House Guest

When Officer Warren counted off all the electronic or battery-powered devices, the one that he did not find was a T.V. remote control. It would have been impossible for a bedridden man to operate a ceiling-mounted T.V. without a remote control.

The last person claiming to see the victim alive was Dr. Yancy. Officer Warren theorized that the doctor killed his uncle before exiting the bedroom. He then took the remote control, left the house, and sneaked around to Uncle Ben's window. By using the remote from outside the locked window, Dr. Yancy was able to give the impression that Uncle Ben was still alive.

The Suicidal Schemer

The captain noticed the victim's folded hands. Since Archer would have died almost instantly, he could not possibly have folded his hands after shooting himself.

The most likely suspect is the doctor. The secretary's comment about Archer's cold, combined with the cough drops, indicate a sore throat. It would have been the easiest thing in the world for Dr. Crocus to volunteer to examine Archer's throat. When confronted with a doctor inches from his face, Archer, like the rest of us, simply closed his eyes. Say "ah."

Super Bowl Madness

The poison couldn't have been in the communal snack food. It must have been in the victim's drink. But Sonny tasted his father's highball right before the game and showed no ill effects.

The only possibility left was the ice. Marie had added poisoned ice cubes to her husband's glass. The fast-acting poison melted as he drank, killing him almost a half-hour after his wife had mixed the deadly highball. While Vince lay gasping for air, his wife was in the kitchen, cleaning the glass of any telltale residue.

The Telltale Prints

The footprints aren't a vital clue. If Aeriel had been killed before the rain started at 2 A.M., anyone could have done it and not left prints. The significant prints are the ones on the acrobat's throat.

The officer noted that the handprints around her neck were backwards and upside down. The killer had strangled Aeriel from above her head, as she was facing away. This is a nearly impossible position—unless you happen to be an acrobat. Rudolph, a jealous suitor, grabbed her around the throat just as they were practicing a new balancing trick for their act.

A Theatrical Threat

When the note arrived, the news of Sir Mortimer's departure was still a secret. That reduced the suspects to five: the producer, the co-star, the wife, the reporter, and Sir Mortimer himself.

The language of the death threat held the pivotal clues. The use of "theater" instead of "theatre," "dishonor" instead of "dishonour," and "trunk" instead of the British term "boot" all show that it had been written by an American.

The star's wife confessed. She sent the note, without Sir Mortimer's knowledge, as a publicity stunt.

The Three Stoogles

Eugene Stoogle testified that the sprinkler system had gone on. But this was impossible. The electricity was still off.

Eugene had arrived first, well before the shower, and parked in the rear, out of sight. During the storm, he confronted his uncle in the old man's bathroom. Their argument culminated in murder. Afterwards, Eugene sneaked down the back stairs and pretended to have just arrived. Knowing the sprinklers would soon go on, as soon as the power was restored, he invented a story in order to explain why his convertible's interior was wet.

Three Weak Alibis

Ellen Youst. It would have been nearly impossible for Ellen to work on her computer while bright sunshine was falling on the screen. She must have left her office while the sky was still cloudy and not returned until shortly before the guard arrived to interview her.

A Timely Alibi

The detective's wife had noticed Juan Garcia's overtime. Why would a man working an eight-hour shift get an hour's worth of overtime? That's why she asked about the date and time of the murder.

The last Sunday in October is when most parts of the United States switch from daylight saving time to standard time. When the clock struck two that morning, it was suddenly one o'clock again. The extra hour affected only one alibi. Instead of having one free hour, Johnny "Dum-Dum" Falco now had two, plenty of time to get from the Tropicana to the victim's house and then to the tavern.

Tornado Allie

The neat, round drops of blood indicate that Allie had been hit while there was little if any wind. Otherwise, the drops would have been blown into a long spray pattern on the ground. Since the wind was still blowing strong when Beth discovered the body, this means that Allie had been attacked before the wind started, certainly before the tornado passed by.

Uncle Nate must be lying. Allie couldn't have left his house after the wind picked up. By that time she was already dead.

Two Places at Once

Frank couldn't be the killer. And yet, the tire treads and the discarded ticket pointed right at him. Since Frank's brothers shared the same motive and the same opportunity, the chief reasoned that one of them killed Gregor and was trying to pin it on Frank.

How did Frank know that the store receipts would still be in the register on that particular night? Emil, the chief recalled, was a teller at the town's only bank. He mentioned to Frank that the hardware store manager had not come in that day, knowing that Frank couldn't resist such an easy score. While Frank was out robbing, Emil was out killing.

When the police found the clues and arrested Frank, Emil figured that his brother would be without an alibi. He never figured on Frank being caught.

The Vandalizing Visitor

The officer was struck by the fact that the second suspect, Mr. Brier, had used a pay phone to call his room instead of one of the courtesy phones. When a service technician from the telephone company opened the phone's coin box, he found a rare old quarter. Mr. Brier had stolen the quarter from the display case. Using the pay phone was the only way he could think of to get rid of the incriminating coin.

The Vanishing Love Token

Inspector Clyde had noticed the full decanter of port. Since the men had been drinking port, the container should have been at least partly empty. With all his wealthy friends watching, Clyde took the decanter to a bathroom sink, poured out the costly port, and revealed the red necklace inside.

The butler eventually confessed. While everyone's attention had been diverted by the billboard, he lifted the necklace and deposited it in the decanter. The crystal pattern and the color of the port make the presence of the necklace undetectable.

The Videotaped Suspect

The videotape showed Al Cuellar closing the apartment door and adjusting his ring. Clearly, he wasn't wearing gloves. And yet the only prints found on the door belonged to the deceased. The explanation was simple enough: Marcus Tomby and Al Cuellar were the same person. And he died of natural causes.

The discovery of a red wig and beard in Tomby's office confirmed this. Marcus had gone undercover at Metro Carting, disguising himself as a new employee, Al Cuellar, in order to get his exposé.

Welcome Back, Cutter

The glass shard reminded the sergeant of the shattered picture glass in the victim's bedroom. The suitcase must have been lying open during the deadly fight. This made him suspect Broderick, who'd testified that Reece had finished unpacking while they were together.

Broderick eventually confessed. That evening he told Reece the reason Marjorie wanted a divorce—she and Broderick were in love. The brothers fought and Reece wound up getting the long end of the sword.

In order to give himself an alibi, Broderick finished unpacking Reece's suitcase. A half-hour later, when he arrived at work, he telephone Parcheesi Pizza, pretending to be his brother.

Which Dewdit Did It?

It was a simple process of elimination. The lawyer knew that Asa had not recently used the back stairs, because of the unbroken spider web. He also couldn't have used the main stairs, not without being seen by Cecil, who claimed to be in the front hall.

Bebe couldn't have entered or left by the kitchen door, not without leaving prints on the recently mopped marble floor.

Therefore, it had to be Cecil.

Who Killed Santa Claus?

Sam Petrie. By leaving the gun on the table, the detective made the unspoken implication that Rudolph had been shot. And yet in Sam's statement, he mentioned the fact that Rudolph had been hit. The only way Sam could have known that was if he had done it himself.

After work on Christmas Eve, Sam stayed behind to turn in his elf costume and pick up his paycheck. He and Rudolph got into one last argument. Rudolph threatened Sam and pulled a gun. In a fit of rage, Sam tore the gun from Rudolph's hand and bashed him over the head.

A Winter's Tale

Julie Becker had been one of the first to arrive. She also claimed never to have gone outside. And yet, when she went to retrieve her coat, it was right on top of the rack.

The chief quickly discovered the truth. At a moment when no one was in the entry hall, Julie had slipped on her coat, grabbed the vase, and rushed outside, hiding the stolen item in a hollow tree stump two blocks away. Julie was back at the party before anyone knew the difference.

INDEX

Solutions appear in italics.

Agent Brown's Shining Moment, 10, *301*

Airport Insecurity, 146, *301*

Alibi at Sea, 298, *302*

Archie's Christmas Surprise, 67, *303*

Around-the-Clock Murder, 235, *303*

An Attack of Gas, 99, *304*

The Bad Samaritan, 211, *305*

The Brothers Ilirium, 136, *305*

Bye-Bye, Bully, 181, *306*

Chili con Carnage, 200, *307*

A Chinese Lie Detector, 133, *307*

The Clumsy Thief, 258, *308*

The Coach's Last Play, 48, *308*

The Convent Mystery, 106, *309*

Dead-End Stoolie, 290, *310*

Death by Chocolate, 110, *310*

Death in the Woods, 278, *311*

Death of a Deceiver, 26, *311*

The Dirty Cop, 59, *312*

Driven to Suicide, 242, *313*

The Emery Emerald, 207, *313*

Even Hypochondriacs Die, 246, *314*

Eye Spy, 89, *314*

The Flat Motorist, 254, *315*

Fooling the Foolproof Alarm, 274, *316*

Friends at the Office, 22, *316*

Good-Neighbor Policy, 81, *317*

The Gypsy Thief, 196, *317*

Hand in the Cookie Jar, 231, *318*

A Hard Day's Night, 167, *319*

High-Rise Homicide, 44, *319*

A Housewarming Theft, 217, *320*

An Inside Job, 102, *320*

The Kidnapping Killer, 192, *321*

Killer Camp Food, 85, *322*

A Lapse in Security, 294, *322*

The Last Poker Hand, 74, *323*

The Locked Room, 125, *324*

Long-Distance Murder, 52, *324*

Looking for a Lookout, 41, *325*

A Maid-Made Discovery, 270, *325*

Maria's Last Clue, 185, *326*

Murder Works Overtime, 282, *327*

Myra's Three Sons, 170, *327*

A Nun Too Pretty Murder, 173, *328*

The Nutty Strangler, 228, *328*

The Party's Over, 30, *329*

The Penguin House Murder, 250, *329*

The Piney Bluffers, 92, *330*

The Playboy's Empty Vase, 203, *331*

Postgraduate Murder, 71, *331*

The Pretender' Ball, 77, *332*

The Pretenders' Ball, II, 149, *332*

The Pretenders' Ball, III, 224, *333*

The Pretenders' Ball, IV, 239, *333*

The Pre-Valentine's Day Murder, 139, *334*

A Quali-Tee Theft, 114, *334*

The Queen Glendora Photos, 55, *335*

A Real False Alarm, 143, *335*

The Shortcut Robbery, 122, *336*

The Smuggler and the Clever Wife, 33, *337*

The Stolen Cleopatra, 63, *337*

Strangulation Station, 156, *338*

The Suicidal House Guest, 37, *339*

The Suicidal Schemer, 160, *339*

Super Bowl Madness, 14, *340*

The Telltale Prints, 188, *341*

A Theatrical Threat, 163, *341*

The Three Stoogles, 118, *342*

Three Weak Alibis, 177, *343*

A Timely Alibi, 129, *343*

Tornado Allie, 214, *344*

Two Places at Once, 286, *344*

The Vandalizing Visitor, 95, *345*

The Vanishing Love Token, 18, *346*

The Videotaped Suspect, 266, *346*

Welcome Back, Cutter, 262, *347*

Which Dewdit Did It?, 220, *348*

Whodunit Solutions, *301*

Who Killed Santa Claus?, 7, *348*

A Winter's Tale, 152, *349*